Models,

Metaphors, and

Intuition

How we think, learn and communicate

Michael Ruhl Frank, Ph.D.

Dedication

To my wife Vicky: The unwavering support, love, and patience you've given me, and the inspiration you've brought me, have made this endeavor possible. With deep appreciation for your presence in my life and the journey we continue to travel together, I dedicate this book to you.

Table of Contents

Prologue

Toward a means for common understanding.

I have no formal training in the world's religions or psychology, and only elementary courses in philosophy. I also have no formal training in neuroscience. This writing is not intended to be a scientific or philosophical offering, but is rather the personal observations and opinions of a scientist. My formal education is in theoretical physics accompanied by a healthy dose of mathematics and computer science. The only real relevance of my training to this writing is that I would consider myself an observer of life or nature, and have a passion for understanding and describing it as simply as I can.

My intent is, therefore, to approach the topics in this book with a mind toward Occam's razor – the simplest explanations are most likely correct. I'll also attempt to make simple connections with your experiences by sharing my own, but will as much as possible limit my storytelling to making those connections in order to illustrate a point. I'll be intentionally brief.

3

I've had the opportunity to pursue several careers in my life – chef, theoretical physicist, vice president at a major aerospace company, and now, with any luck, a writer. I've always considered myself a bit of a dabbler. I'm fascinated by many things, curious, and either courageous or foolish enough to think I could do them. I've lived in most regions of the United States and have traveled a substantial portion of the world. In short, I've lived – courageously – tried and failed at many things and occasionally, largely due to luck and timing, succeeded at a few. And I would say I've done this living with a background level of fear overcome only by a drive to improve myself through experiences and thereby increase my own worth.

I discovered at a young age that life was impermanent. Maybe through losing loved ones, or witnessing tragedy, or seeing scenes of death on television, I came to the conclusion that I too will one day die. I found it hard to sleep at night for many years after, and sometimes I still do.

It's through this background of fear confronted by the desire to be more somehow, and my observations of life in general, that I've come to the conclusion that the fundamental motives of all animals are self preservation and self actualization or more simply, fear and desire.[1] For most animals, self actualization amounts to reproduction (propagation of the species) and self preservation is, therefore, the primary driver. We humans have the capacity for much more, and should hold ourselves to much higher standards. "Self" preservation is "hard wired" in our brains, but we can consciously adjust our thinking to encompass a broader sense of self – both in our preservation and in our collective actualization.

My goal in this writing is to promote *social consciousness* and increase awareness and understanding of the "human condition" that we all share, and that ultimately binds us all in our future, and our fate. I endeavor to pursue that goal with a series of discussions on *how we think, how we learn, and how we communicate* against the backdrop of our own individual consciousness, and to do so in an accessible manner. These discussions will leverage similarities of the human brain to neural networks in computing and artificial intelligence – as it has become increasingly important recently to understand these concepts. Finally, with hope and humility, I offer my perspective on a path toward improvement going forward.

I should point out here that I've used the term "consciousness" in two different ways – one being akin to awareness (e.g., social consciousness), the other (harder to define) being individual subjective experience.[2] And although I don't intend this to be a rigorous philosophical writing, I'd like to be at least somewhat mindful of the difference as I consider it to be among the more fundamental questions facing humankind. So what I would offer regarding consciousness as subjective experience is this: You might be the most knowledgeable person in the history of the world about crows, but you don't know what it "feels like" to be a crow – "see" through a crow's eyes, hear a crow's thoughts, feel a crow's fears and affections.

Throughout the remainder of this work, I'll try to be explicit in my meaning, if it's not obvious, and will focus on what it "feels like" to be a conscious human. We each uniquely experience our "selves" – not just our bodily sensations, but also things like thoughts, hopes, dreams, and

6

emotions. What's common is the fact that *we do.* It's what I consider to be our shared humanity.

Finally, the one caveat I'd like to make is that, throughout this book, you're getting my opinion based on the background I've provided above. Whether right or wrong, it's just opinion. It's up to you to decide if it has any value or meaning. My hope is to provoke thought and maybe some improvement.

Introduction – establishing a baseline

It's difficult to navigate the path ahead by looking in the rear-view mirror.

Evolution does not anticipate the future, but is rather governed by present and past conditions. A random variant survives based on its ability to adapt to the current environment, and the environment's adoption of it. The current environment is, of course, the product of previous applications of this process, which we can trace back through time. This is an iterative process where the next iteration depends on the previous. However, as any student of regression analysis will attest, extrapolation of the past into the future assumes that future conditions very closely resemble the past, which in the presence of rapid change is likely a bad assumption.

Our technology is exploding faster than the evolutionary processes governing our culture can achieve. Using Moore's Law[3] as a benchmark for technology change implies a biennial pace of significant change. Biological evolution, on the other hand, happens at a scale of thousands or even millions of years. And although measuring cultural evolution or major cultural change is complicated, I would argue that it is at least multigenerational, and therefore on the order of a hundred or so years. In today's world, we are consequently under constant pressure to adapt to new technologies without understanding the cultural implications.

So technology is driving our culture. Yet, in spite of global communication for example, we still largely operate in tribes – countries, races, religions, political parties, economic classes – that are focused on the betterment of their own at the exclusion of others rather than the survival and betterment of the whole. And many of those tribes now have the technological capability to destroy the whole. The accumulation of knowledge from one generation to the next is very visible in technology and science, but not as much in the knowledge of how to live well with ourselves and others – peaceful, compassionate, comfortable. Our thinking, understanding, and cultural norms must keep pace with our technological advances.

The human race and our magnificent brains may have evolved quite by accident. As our ancestors began walking upright in the heat of the savannas, their brains evolved an increased layer of adaptive neurons (neocortex) that served to both protect and replace neurons that might perish as a result of heat stroke (R. Ornstein, 1992, Chapter 6).[4] This led to accelerated growth in brain size, and the adaptive capability and level of consciousness that makes humans so unique.

In modern times, as we've adapted to all climate conditions, that excess brain capacity has given us a wealth of technological advances, but our cultural evolution beyond tribal rivalries seems to have lagged significantly behind. In any case, we need to find a way to work together to avert our own self-destruction, and in my opinion understanding how we think, learn, and communicate is the key.

In general terms, communication is an essential evolutionary element. In order for a collection of individual "things" to become one coherent "thing" operating as a collective, communication must occur. In the simplest case, communication via chemical exchange facilitates a collection of solitary cells transitioning to a multi-cellular organism where each component has a negotiated role, perhaps based on proximity, that has evolved to benefit the whole. This evolution led to the development of a central nervous system and arguably to consciousness.

On a larger scale, the advent of goal-oriented thinking, learning, and communicating allowed nomadic hunter gatherers to transition to collective agriculturalists. By working together to modify the environment, their survival became easier. This negotiated set of roles and hierarchy eventually enabled the Neolithic Revolution. In that case, communication and the development of a culture provided the basis for things like centralized administrations and political structures, hierarchical ideologies, depersonalized systems of knowledge (e.g. writing), densely populated settlements, specialization and division of labor, trade, and art.

There seems to be some "tipping point" that must be reached for these transitions to occur. Somehow the whole becomes preferential to the sum of the parts. It might be the response to a common threat to survival or a relatively random event that leads to greater success and the model or variant therefore spreads. Like the path of least resistance, somehow survival becomes easier or more secure. *Natural selection applies to everything.*

The same is becoming increasingly true today for the various nations of the world. Collaboration and cooperation lead to increased security and efficiency. Although we've taken a step back recently with the spread of nationalism, it appears we are at a tipping point of sorts. With our technology, both the ability to access the world through communication in the palm of our hands and the ability of a single, even isolated, nation to effectively destroy human existence has placed us at this point. As soon as one isolated group has the ability to impact the whole, we have a collective threat to our existence.

It is not possible, in my opinion, to retreat from the global nature of our existence. To do so would lead to ongoing wars between those who "have" trying to protect their gains from those who "don't have" in their efforts to gain more. And out of increasing desperation, destruction of the whole becomes increasingly likely. We must find a way to adapt our many global cultures to a future global society. Cultural adaptation starts with communication.

So how does communication work?

When you read the word cat, or dog, or house, or car, you likely "see" images in your head. Words are "pointers" to concepts or symbols. When I hear the word "cat", for example, I see an image of our kitty Sammie (a Chocolate-Point Himalayan), and fondly remember how she'd wake me in the morning with a gentle purr followed by the clanging of her food dish when I didn't respond promptly.

When you read the words love, or joy, or frustration, or sadness, you likely play "episodes" in your mind like short movies of the experiences that these words symbolize to you. When I think of joy, I visualize the time I spend with my wife Vicky laughing about the silly sense of humor we share. When I think of sadness, I remember the passing of my parents and how hard it was to deliver their eulogies.

These symbols and episodic memories provide us with *metaphors* that we use to relate with other people and their experiences. Here I use the term metaphor because, as we'll explore more later, the brain doesn't capture 100% of the reality we live in, but provides us with a representation based on our "need to know". It is through these metaphors that we experience the world around us – subjectively – as opposed to simply processing data.

The exchange of words, whether verbally or written, relates to a series of symbols – metaphors – in our minds that provide us with meaning. If we have no metaphor developed from a prior experience for a particular word, or our experiences and corresponding metaphors don't match, then it is difficult to relate with each other and communication can break down. These metaphors are dynamic and continuously evolve as we encounter new experiences.

The dance of symbols in our minds as we think and relate experiences is equally represented by patterns and sequences of neurons activating. These are two levels of description for the same phenomenon – symbols, images, or metaphors operating in our minds and neurons activating in our brains. Our interest here is more with the former than the latter, but the mechanism that allows electrical impulses to generate images in our minds is both fascinating and a fundamental ingredient in how we process the sense data we receive both consciously and subconsciously. I will continue to use *brain* in reference to the physical processes of neurons and *mind* in reference to the abstraction of mental images and associated structure. Some authors also liken this distinction to the hardware and software respectively operating on your computer.

Our experiences are further not limited to our external senses. We are also the author, narrator, and audience for the "movie" playing in our heads. We are in a recursive, level-crossing, causal relationship with ourselves.

I am authoring, performing in, narrating, and viewing the movie in my head. It is my "feeling" of consciousness.

In Douglas Hofstadter's book, "I am a strange loop,"[5] Hofstadter uses Escher's "Drawing Hands" to help illustrate this idea. Hofstadter explores the question of consciousness and postulates a connection to recursive processes that are level-crossing in the sense of levels of description or abstraction. He further raises the question of the future ability of computers, through artificial intelligence (AI), to develop consciousness.

Conversely, Christof Koch, in his book, "The Feeling of Life Itself: Why Consciousness Is Widespread but Can't Be Computed,"[6] also explores consciousness and adds that causality is a fundamental ingredient. He employs a model known as the Integrated Information Theory (IIT) to examine the ability of computing systems to achieve consciousness.

Finally, Michael S. A. Graziano in his book "Rethinking Consciousness: A Scientific Theory of Subjective Experience"[7] takes the view that the key to consciousness is attention – the ability of the brain to focus its limited resources on a restricted piece of the world at any one time in order to process it in greater depth. Graziano further elaborates on this idea through the development of an *attention schema*, which is a bundle of information that describes attention – not the object being attended, but attention itself.

Our minds utilize this attention schema to monitor the state of attention, keep track of how it can change dynamically from state to state, and predict how it may change in the next few moments. It is an ancient, highly simplified, internal model, honed by evolution to serve two main useful functions. Its first function is as a self model, to monitor, make predictions about, and help control our own attention. The second function is as a catalyst for social cognition, allowing us to model the attentional states of others and thus predict their behavior.

Simply put, in order to control my "self" – my focus, attention, thoughts – I must have an internal *model* of "myself". This model is the lead role in my movie. And in order to predict the behavior of others, which would appear to be preferential from an evolutionary sense, I must have a model of them.

These are but a few of the many models and explanations for what consciousness is, and they appear to be more similar than different. Our interest here is more about how we experience consciousness in our minds, rather than a specific mechanism. Although how we experience consciousness may provide some useful insights. Further, whether AI leads to consciousness or not is not our concern here, but is rather that, we, as conscious beings, need to come to grips with our consciousness and the preservation and further development of this gift.

As I write this book, I am recalling ideas and thoughts that I've cataloged over time, and in the process of their merging as text onto my computer, new ideas are generated. All of this is happening inside my head.

The dialogue in my head has a causal impact on my life as well:

I am the creator of the self that I am.

We have developed the capability for "self creation". For example, on reflection of the events of a day or conversations, I have the opportunity to assess how I behaved (introspection) and to make a conscious effort to adjust my "self model" in the future. Although our basic wiring is embedded in our subconscious reactions, we have, nonetheless, the ability through our own conscious observation and adaptation to overcome our evolutionary programming.

Our brain wiring is the result of millions of years of evolution, and has to a large extent centered around reacting to immediate threats versus long-term strategic planning. However, threats to our existence are no longer immediate things like being eaten by other animals, but are rather broader, longer-term things like war, famine, pandemics, overpopulation, and global warming. Our survival problems are becoming more and more collective and global rather than individual and local.

Part of the challenge of addressing these threats is that our individual time horizons are based on our lifetimes. The common thinking is "when this problem becomes critical, I'll be dead and gone." We appear to have "generational amnesia". We tend to repeat the same cultural mistakes because of our relatively short time horizons and our failure to learn and document cultural lessons as opposed to our well-documented learning of science and technology. This appears to be a value proposition. Cultural improvements don't typically garner recognition and monetary rewards. As an aside, If you want to know what someone values, you should look at their bank account and their calendar. It's how they spend their money and their time.

Value propositions are best described in the study of economics, which I consider to be a study of incentives and behavior. If we want to effect large-scale changes in behaviors, we need to somehow address our economic models – incentives. Monetarily, a tree is worth more dead than alive, as is a whale, or other resources we consume. We are *consumers,* and our attention has monetary value to the sellers of goods and services. They are cultivating attention for profit. As we'll explore more later in *how we communicate,* television and internet media are, for example, designed to grab, hold, and direct our attention to be used to shape our consumption.

Additionally, in many parts of the world day-to-day survival (self preservation) is still the dominant reality. Long-term strategic planning (self actualization) seems irrelevant if you can't pay your rent or feed yourself and your family today. The current trend toward worsening economic inequality presents significant roadblocks to attaining a sense of common values and goals.

Finally, in more developed areas, children today have access to information through their "smart phones" and televisions that they're not mentally or emotionally equipped to manage. These influences affect their developing minds both conscious and subconscious. And at a larger scale, they will then carry these influences into our societal norms and culture. We've come to accept violence and a "reality-TV" role model of appropriate behavior. We self-segregate into groups that are "like" ourselves – religion, race, political party, area of town or country. And as we group ourselves, we look at "others" as somehow lesser. We all carry conscious or unconscious biases that influence our reactions and decisions.

The worst things that happen in the world come from one human being seeing another human being as less than human.

Why are some people successful and others less so – seemingly regardless of their intelligence or talent? When we say someone is "bright", what do we mean? There are unconscious or subconscious signals that we send and receive that lead us to conclusions that are conditioned responses based on both our evolutionary wiring and our environmental exposure. Can we develop more ability to tap into those signals and develop more "self-awareness"? Why would we want to do that?

Toward a means for common understanding

Reality is nothing more than an agreed to set of perceptions built upon past experiences.

The discourse of my view versus your view and who is most right is symptomatic of our limited worldview. We are limited by our own body of experience and familiar culture. It is the filter through which we view the world. Our perception of the world around us is dependent on our brain's interpretation, or *model* of the sense data we receive. The process of forming that model in turn involves a series of comparisons with established symbols in our mind. If my experience model and my corresponding set of metaphors don't match yours, then we could have very different perceptions of the same event. The more important question is how do we establish a common view.

Our minds' use of models and metaphors as a method of communication is both rich as a means of reaching understanding, and fraught with peril as a means of manipulation. Our own intuition may be full of brilliant insights, but also subject to bias instilled in us from our experience or cultural history.

This book endeavors to explore these concepts in order to establish a knowledge base for common language and understanding. It is born out of my empathy and compassion for others, and my desire to help ease the fear and increase the joy of living – help folks live a more comfortable life and maybe indirectly help people become more collectively actualized through their understanding and compassion for others.

We are all faced with the human condition. We are all blessed and cursed with the knowledge that we each will one day face death. Whether death is a transition to another state of consciousness or an end, it is, to me at least, a gnawing uncertainty, and is pervasive in almost everything I do. I personally somehow find comfort in understanding, and my hope is that this book will help bring comfort in understanding, empathy, and compassion to others.

I believe we're all seeking comfort, security, and reassurance. I was working in the yard one day and I could hear a church service in the distance. It was summertime and the service was outdoors with amplified music. The lyrics of the music offered the reassurance that if you followed the teaching espoused, then you would be rewarded with an afterlife. This is the basis for many religions – the promise of something more if you live in a particular way. And the something they're promising is relief from the thing we fear most. One of the problems is that they don't agree on what is the "right" way to live, and are willing to wage war to force their way on others.

This is not a critique of religion or faith, but rather a caution of those who administer it. Offering comfort in exchange for living a righteous life is probably not a bad thing. My caution is who gets to define what a righteous life is and what their motives are. If it excludes anyone, or promotes bias, or promotes harm to anyone, or provides exorbitant profits to its administrators, there is a problem.

For the record, I consider myself a spiritual person who is open to the possibility of a greater reality (more on that in the epilogue). Throughout my life I've sought out teachers or gurus who could offer me reassurance only to find that they were as much searching and/or as deeply troubled as me; or worse yet, frauds. My concern is that our fears are sometimes used as a means of manipulation and exclusion.

I'd like to now bring our introduction to a close by defining a few terms that we'll be using throughout this book – common language facilitates common understanding.

Models

All models are wrong, some models are useful.

A model is a graphical, mathematical (symbolic), physical, or verbal representation or simplified version of a concept, phenomenon, relationship, structure, system, or an aspect of the real world. The objectives of a model include (1) to facilitate understanding by eliminating unnecessary components, (2) to aid in decision making by simulating "what if" scenarios, (3) to explain, control, and predict events on the basis of past observations. Since most objects and phenomenon are very complicated (have numerous parts) and much too complex (parts have dense interconnections) to be comprehended in their entirety, *a model contains only those features that are of primary importance to the model maker's purpose.* Hence the statement at the beginning of this section – all models are wrong, in some sense, by definition. *Something that we all need to come to grips with is that the brain is a modeler...*

Our consciously perceived reality is produced by our subconscious brain and the selective processing and interpretation of sense data. These processes are the result of our evolutionary history and have generally served us well. The subconscious brain as a model maker, and our sense-data collection apparatus, serves the conscious mind by not overwhelming it with data, but providing it with the necessary information for the sake of decision making – the need to know. We in fact, maintain a continually evolving model of ourselves and when we're talking with someone, we produce a model of that person and project that image of them onto our dialogue – our model of who they are and their intentions color our reactions.

Looking forward, however, it will likely become increasingly important for us to recognize the role of these processes and how they influence or bias our decisions – potentially to our detriment.

Metaphors

All the world's a stage...

Metaphors are linguistic devices that enrich our communication by drawing comparisons between two seemingly unrelated concepts, often to convey abstract or complex ideas in more accessible terms. They serve as powerful tools for evoking imagery and emotion in language. Metaphors allow us to understand unfamiliar concepts by relating them to familiar ones, making them an essential component of poetry, literature, and everyday language. However, while they enhance expression, metaphors can also introduce ambiguity if not used judiciously, as their interpretation may vary from person to person. Metaphors are like colorful threads woven into the fabric of language, illuminating our thoughts and expressions with vivid connections between the known and the mysterious.

My use of the term metaphor here is to illustrate the relationship between things like objects, feelings, or events and the corresponding representations formed in our minds. These representations as a collection form the basis for our communication and understanding.

Words are links or "pointers" to these metaphors. The ability to communicate in multiple languages amounts to the ability to establish multiple pointers to the same metaphor. If we were to attempt communication directly through metaphors, we would quickly realize that common experiences are essential for common understanding.

I am reminded of a Star Trek episode[8] in which Captain Picard is transported against his will to an alien planet where he is to engage in battle against a monster foe. Also joining Picard is the captain of another ship who was responsible for transporting Picard to the planet, and who only communicates in metaphors. Unbeknownst to Picard, the other captain is there to help him defeat the monster, and by doing so create a common experience and bond between their peoples. I won't spoil the ending, but suffice it to say that, although difficult because of the lack of a shared culture, Picard learns to communicate through metaphors.

Intuition

On exactly one night in its entire lifetime, the yucca moth discovers pollen in the opened flowers of the yucca plant, forms some into a pellet, and then transports this pellet, with one of its eggs, to the pistil of another yucca plant. This activity cannot be "learned" it makes more sense to describe the yucca moth as experiencing intuition about how to act.[9]

Intuition is the ability to acquire knowledge without proof, evidence, or conscious reasoning, or without understanding how the knowledge was acquired.

Intuition, often referred to as our "gut feeling" or instinct, is a remarkable facet of human cognition. It represents our ability to make rapid, subconscious judgments or decisions based on a wealth of past experiences, knowledge, and patterns that our brain has absorbed over time. It's the inexplicable sense that guides us when facing uncertainty or complexity, providing valuable insights and guidance even when we can't explicitly explain our choices. Intuition can be a powerful ally, leading to creative solutions and quick assessments, but it can also be fallible, occasionally leading us astray when emotions or biases cloud our judgment. In essence, intuition is a fascinating interplay between our conscious and unconscious minds, a mysterious force that influences our decision-making in ways that science is still unraveling.

Different writers give the word "intuition" a variety of different meanings, ranging from direct access to unconscious knowledge, unconscious cognition, inner sensing, inner insight to unconscious pattern-recognition and the ability to understand something instinctively, without the need for conscious reasoning. The key point is that, in each of these, some access to unconscious processes has materialized at a conscious level.

I'm sure many of us have had the experience of concentrating for a long period of time on a problem and walking away empty handed only to have the solution "pop" into our minds at a later point during relaxation or even sleep. I've often found taking a walk and allowing my mind to wander produced better results than relentless concentration.

I'm reminded of the story of Archimedes where the king gives him the task of proving that his intricately ornate crown is made entirely of gold and not plated (implying the metalsmith substituted lead for gold and kept the gold). Knowing the density of gold (weight/volume), Archimedes only needed to weigh the crown and calculate the volume. But how to calculate the volume of an intricate object? After puzzling for some time, the story goes that Archimedes decided to take a break at the public bath. As he sat in the tub, water spilled out over the edge and – eureka! – the answer hit him. *The volume of water displaced by a submerged object is equal to the volume of the object.* And hence we have the basis for Archimedes principle (relies on the fact that water is incompressible). The rest of the story is that, in his excitement, Archimedes ran naked through the streets, but that's likely embellishment. The point is that by quieting the conscious mind the subconscious mind can be heard, and may provide valuable insights.

How do we become more aware?

The following three sections – how we think, how we learn, and how we communicate – are what I believe to be foundational to understanding human nature – the human condition. My hope is that through this understanding we will develop more awareness and compassion for ourselves and others.

How we think

I am, I exist...I am a thing that thinks – AKA, I think therefore I am.

Descartes, in his "Meditations on First Philosophy",[10] describes the ability to doubt all aspects of physical reality and is left with only one thing he cannot doubt – his own existence. For to do so would be a logical contradiction. He therefore comes to the conclusion that he exists, as is demonstrated by the fact that he is thinking. His awareness of his thinking – the ability to "hear" his own thoughts – is a statement of consciousness. As I stated in the introduction, *I am authoring, performing in, narrating, and viewing the movie in my head.* Descartes then goes on to infer the existence of extended reality and god.

We could just as easily infer that extended reality doesn't exist at all since all of our experience of the external universe comes to our brains via sense data. And when I say "external universe" I mean to include our physical bodies as well. We could in fact be conscious residents in an elaborate "computer" simulation.[11] As an aside, this would put an interesting twist on the "body-mind problem" that philosophers have wrestled with for some time.[12] If there is no "body", the problem presumably goes away. The potential of consciousness to be uploaded into a computer simulation has been explored in some detail,[13] and it could be argued that it *is* our reality. We could, if fact, argue that everything we've experienced up to now are only memories implanted in our brains and didn't actually occur at all. We simply cannot *prove* anything beyond our own existence.

I won't attempt to draw any conclusions about the ultimate reality, but will instead embrace the reality we appear to be in and move on from there. I spent a significant portion of my life studying and practicing theoretical physics and, although the more I learned the more I discovered how much we don't know, I'm not quite ready to abandon the idea that the physical universe exists, and that historical cause and effect has landed us in the here and now.

So, let's assume the physical universe that we appear to dwell in, as well the inhabitants – like you and me, and maybe a few others – actually does exist. We then experience and interpret (perceive) this reality through our senses and our internal processes.

Perception can generally be split into two processes:

(1) Mechanical processing of sensory input, which transforms low-level data into higher-level information (e.g., extracting shapes for object recognition);

(2) Interpretive processing – *thought*, which is connected with a person's concepts and expectations (models and metaphors), and selective mechanisms (such as attention) that influence perception. This processing may or may not involve physical sense data; i.e., it could be based on introspection – how I perceive and interpret my own thoughts – my "self" model.

Perception depends on complex functions of our brains and is subjective in general because of the capabilities of our sensing apparatus, and in particular because of our library of individual experiences – our individual set of metaphors and models.

The goal in the following sections is to build from the mechanical processing of the brain through layers of abstraction to the imagery of the mind. I'll use analogies from the world of computing to help illustrate the journey. I'll begin with a simplistic description of brain dynamics by using a model of neural networks. Then continuing with the computing analogy, I'll explore the layers of abstraction built up in software to higher-level descriptions like object-oriented modeling. Finally, I'll use this framework to describe an operating model of how we think – what is thought and how consciousness might arise. Like all models, as pointed out previously, our discussion here will necessarily be simplified and incomplete.

Chances are when you use your computer, your interest and attention is focused on the images on your screen rather than the operation of the software that creates those images or the circuitry upon which the software executes. This is likely also the case with your mind – we don't choose which neurons are activated in our brains when we think of cat or joy, we simply "see" images and "feel" emotions in our minds. These are likely the same neurons or patterns of neurons, by the way, that were activated when we "saw" the original image or "felt" the original emotion. Our interest here, however, is to attempt to understand the brain and mind at a somewhat deeper level with the goal of understanding our humanity, and through that understanding, encourage compassion for both ourselves and others.

From neurons and synapses...

Neural networks in computing largely consist of two constructs – nodes (analogous to neurons) and weight factors (analogous to synapses). Nodes are connected to other nodes via the weight factors. Two things happen within a node. First, the input from other nodes is multiplied by their respective weight factors and all of these products are summed to form one overall "weighted-average" input. Second, this overall input is then evaluated against a threshold and a decision is made whether or not to send an output, or how much output to send. This process continues across the layers[14] of the network in one direction in most cases, but can involve recursion.

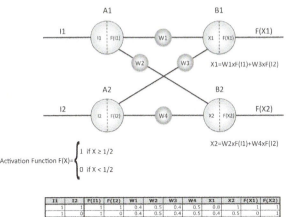

Activation Function $F(X)=\begin{cases}1 & \text{if } X \geq 1/2\\ 0 & \text{if } X < 1/2\end{cases}$

$X2 = W2 \times F(I1) + W4 \times F(I2)$

I1	I2	F(I1)	F(I2)	W1	W2	W3	W4	X1	X2	F(X1)	F(X2)
1	1	1	1	0.4	0.5	0.4	0.5	0.8	1	1	1
1	0	1	0	0.4	0.5	0.4	0.5	0.4	0.5	0	1
0	1	0	1	0.4	0.5	0.4	0.5	0.4	0.5	0	1
0	0	0	0	0.4	0.5	0.4	0.5	0	0	0	0

Figure 1

To illustrate this process, let's consider a simple example of four nodes as shown in Figure 1. I'll describe the process in both mathematics and words to help ensure clarity.

As stated above, each of the nodes (labeled A1, A2, B1, and B2) perform two tasks as indicated by the dividing dashed line. The first task is to evaluate the input (shown as I1, I2, X1, and X2 in the figure). The second is to make the output decision. This occurs via something called an "activation function" (shown as F(X) in the figure). For those unfamiliar with the function notation, it simply means that for a given input number (labeled X) an output number (labeled F(X)) is generated based on a rule. Here the rule (function F(X)) we're using is a "step function", which in this case means that if the input X is greater than or equal to ½, the output is 1. Otherwise, if the input X is less than ½, the output is 0. In this way the node is "activated" or not based on the level of the input.

In the case of nodes A1 and A2, the given inputs are simply I1 and I2 respectively. For B1 and B2 the inputs are calculated as the sum of the products of the outputs of the neighboring nodes and the respective weight factors. So for example the input to B1 (labeled X1 in the figure) is the output of A1 (which is F(I1)) multiplied by the weight factor W1 and added to the output of A2 (which is F(I2)) multiplied by the weight factor W3.

The mathematical details are likely less important to most readers. The important points are that the weight factors determine the relative importance of the information moving from one node to the next, and the nodes make a "decision" to send a signal forward based on the strength of the collective input. It is the adjustment of the weight factors that is reflective of how the network "learns", and is typically achieved through an error-minimization scheme. That is, the result of a pass through the network is compared with the expected result and weight factors are adjusted to improve the accuracy.

The inputs, weight factors, and outputs are shown in the table at the bottom of the figure. Here I've chosen the value of the weight factors to illustrate a point. Namely, by looking at the inputs I1 and I2 you can see that this simple network generates a logical "AND" operation for the output F(X1). Likewise, the network generates a logical "OR" operation for the output F(X2). Why is this important? AND and OR operations form the basis for digital computing, and can be combined to form computer memory storage.[15] So it's easy to see how our brains can operate much like a digital computer.

In neural-network computing applications an activation function is chosen to have some threshold behavior, and the weight factors are allowed to adjust as the network "learns". This is very much like the operation of the brain as well, as we'll discuss more in the next section on how we learn.

One of the better publicized applications of neural networks is facial recognition. The network "learns" characteristic facial features and is able to match them to a data base – a library of stored models. The mechanics of processing sense data in our brains is also largely analogous.

The human brain houses on the order of 100 billion neurons (nodes in our example above) and on the order of a trillion synapses (weight factors in our example). This provides a demonstration of the computing power of the brain. And although here we've chosen a two-state activation function above to illustrate the relationship to digital computing, the fact is that neurons can achieve many-level outputs giving even greater flexibility, and our synapses (weight factors) adjust as we learn and experience the world around and within us. It has even been suggested that there might be a "coherence" derived from quantum-mechanical effects in synaptic responses that could contribute to consciousness.[16]

The sheer number of neurons also illustrates a significant structural challenge in determining how all the neurons are connected to each other. If every neuron was connected to every other neuron, the brain would need to be the size of a house to contain all the connections. Here's the math, with n representing the number of neurons, the number of links would be $n(n - 1)/2$ – a very large number.

The brain solves this problem by using what's called a "small-world" interconnection scheme. Any given neuron is connected to a few thousand other neurons (on average), and the densest connections are to nearby neurons. The small "communities" in the cortex are called minicolumns. Neocortical minicolumns consist of about 100 neurons in a vertical column whose surface area is about 40 square micrometers. This interconnection scheme also becomes important in our discussion of the hierarchy of information management to follow shortly.

From an evolutionary standpoint, as was mentioned in the introduction, single-celled organisms evolved into multicellular organisms through communication – cells in different parts of the organism communicated by releasing certain substances into the spaces between the cells. Some of these substances became neurotransmitters. Organisms that could act coherently by chemical communication were naturally selected. As multicellular organisms became larger and more sophisticated, neurons took over much of the job of communicating from one part of the organism to another. Neural networks were further selected by evolutionary mechanisms as fast ways to optimize communication and coordinated, multicellular action within an organism. In short, random mutations to these systems gave the organism a survival advantage that was passed from one generation to the next. As an aside, our brain development demonstrates the application of a common systems engineering practice – maximize modularity while minimizing interface complexity.

An additional point based on the work of Godel[17] is that all systems can be reduced to integer manipulation – like the workings of digital computers. Our brains, via our neural networks, therefore possess an amazing capacity to model

43

the world around us. But, as we also discussed in the introduction, models are by definition incomplete and our evolution has, to this point, largely focused on survival. Our models have therefore been necessarily biased by their intended purpose.

To object models...

So how do we get from neurons and synapses to object models? It may be more intuitive to answer the question first in reverse – how do we get from object models to neurons and synapses?

In our computing analogy, programs or routines written in higher-level programming languages are either "interpreted" or "compiled" into "machine" language that operates directly with the circuitry. When I refer to higher-level programming languages I mean something that has structure and syntax that makes it at least somewhat "readable". When I say machine language I mean the sequence of ones and zeros that a computer actually executes. Let's consider a few examples.

One of the first computer languages I learned is called FORTRAN (FORmula TRANslation). In general FORTRAN is a structured, "procedural" language in that a FORTRAN program consists of a series of operations that are performed on data to produce an output or result. Like most procedural languages, FORTRAN can perform "loops" of repeated instructions and has logical flow control like, *if a condition is true do this, else do that.* It's a language that's frequently used in scientific computing, and I wrote tens of thousands of lines of code aimed at solving mathematical equations or modeling physical systems. It is a "compiled" language in that it is translated into "machine" language prior to execution. The FORTRAN code itself is transportable – that is, it can be moved to other computers, but it relies on a machine-specific compiler to translate it into something the machine can execute.

I also learned a lower-level language referred to as Assembly. Assembly language is unique to, and works directly with, a given machine's architecture. It therefore does not require compiling or interpreting, but is also not transportable. It performs operations like loading the contents of a memory location into a register and performing "bit" manipulations (the ones and zeros that make your computer work). It is very useful, for example, for interfacing laboratory equipment with computers, but is not generally reflective of the way we think, and is cumbersome in the sheer number of manipulations required to complete a task.

Finally, in the mid-nineteen-nineties a language called Java was developed and object-oriented programming grew in popularity. This was due in large part to Java's portability and use in web-based applications. Java has an intermediate compilation into something called the Java Virtual Machine – "byte code" – that is independent of any specific computer architecture. It then executes in what's called the Java runtime environment that *is* computer dependent, but can be integrated with your web browser. This allowed web developers to to produce much more feature rich and dynamic web-based applications. Java has many visualization "libraries" – a collection of objects and routines – that allow developers to produce visual representations.

Object-oriented programming arguably started sometime in the nineteen-sixties in the early years of artificial intelligence, and is very different from ordinary procedural languages in that the thought process revolves around the modeling of systems as interacting "objects". In this way, object oriented programming more closely relates real-world objects with their digital counterparts.

Objects contain data fields or "attributes" and procedures called "methods". A feature of objects is that an object's procedures can access and even modify the data fields of the object with which they are associated (objects have a notion of "self"). So for example, consider an object like an orange. An orange has attributes like size, color, sweetness, skin thickness, and juiciness. It has methods – things it can do or can be done to it – like grown, eaten, juiced, or maybe thrown. It may also have methods that act on it's own attributes like ripening might increase sweetness and juiciness.

Objects can "inherit" attributes and methods from other objects in a hierarchy. For example, an orange is a type of fruit. In this way we can classify the world around us in terms of a hierarchy of objects. The navel orange in my refrigerator is, for example, a specific instance of a navel orange, which is inherited from the larger class of oranges, which is inherited from the still larger class of fruit,...you get the picture. Further, objects can be composed of other objects. Our orange could be composed of a peel and seeds and pith and pulp. Object-oriented programming is rich in it's ability to model reality in a way that is analogous with how we think and experience reality.

So a programmer working with an object-oriented programming language can design programs in a way that is more aligned with how we "think" – a world of interacting objects that are modeled based on our experience. They don't need to be concerned with how their code looks or operates at the machine level. The compiler or interpreter does that for them. The user of the finished program – like you sitting in front of your computer looking at the images on your screen – doesn't need to be concerned with the high-level code, the compiler, or the operation at the machine level. There are layers of abstraction – a hierarchy of operations, and you – the end user – are interacting with the images on your computer screen.

Its fairly easy to see via these layers of abstraction – through compilation and/or interpretation – how computer programs can go from visual images on your screen to object models to machine language and execution. I would argue that the reverse is largely an equivalent process. Consider a stream of ones and zeros traveling over the internet, arriving at your computer, working its way up through the layers of abstraction we just described, and producing images on your screen.

How we think

Our brains operate much the same way. I don't necessarily mean that our brains contain a compiler, but rather that analogous layers of abstraction provide interpretation of higher level vision to actual execution. When we think about walking, for example, we don't think about which neurons need to activate in order to move which muscles. Instead, we envision at a high level perhaps the direction and speed at which we wish to move, and somewhere in the organizational hierarchy of our brain our walk "routine" is invoked and it activates the appropriate series of neurons. Or when a stream of photons arrives at our eye, a series of events occurs again through layers of abstraction and an image appears in our minds.

So we've identified at least three "layers of abstraction" – one being the physical layer that is neurons activating causing muscles to move or neurons activating as light impinges on receptors, one an object-model / procedural description, and one a high-level vision.

At a subconscious level, our brains build object models of the world around us – our collection of models and metaphors. *Our subconscious brain is an object-oriented programmer.* We classify objects in various ways – like things we can eat, things we should fear, things like us. We even have a model of ourselves. From an evolutionary standpoint these object models provided a survival advantage in the ability to predict an outcome based on prior experience or conditioning built into the models. Our brains are conditioned to predict the near-term future (more on this in the epilogue).

These object models further contain context. Fire, for example, is something that can cause harm, but can also cook our food and provide warmth depending on its use – like "use cases" in object-oriented programming. Context is the information about a particular event involving an object, rather than just the information about the object itself. Context is knowing where or how you learned a particular fact rather than just knowing the fact. Typically the name for contextual memory is episodic memory, that is, memory associated with an event or episode. General memory about facts is called semantic memory. Rich episodic memory is largely considered to be one of the hallmarks of human consciousness because episodic memory involves awareness of oneself in one's particular surroundings at a particular time – a self model.

Further, our brains are truly multitasking – unlike computers with a single central processing unit (CPU) in which processes execute briefly and are swapped out for other processes to give the appearance of multitasking. All of our bodily functions are taking place, for example, without us giving it a conscious thought. However, as much as we'd like to think we can *consciously* multitask, our conscious minds appear to focus on one thing at a time.

One argument to the contrary is the following aside. I once knew an executive assistant who could listen to a recorded dictation, type what she was hearing, answer the phone, and speak to someone approaching her desk without stopping the dictation. I would argue that she found a way to let her subconscious brain listen and type while she consciously performed other tasks. She probably could not tell you what the topic of the dictation was. This ability was developed over time – learned – as we'll discuss more in the next section.

The key point is that our conscious mind doesn't multitask – our attention is directed and can also be distracted. Our subconscious brain *does* multitask and performs a multitude of tasks often without our conscious awareness. How often have you been performing a somewhat mundane daily task while the focus of your attention has been on something else? I have found myself in the shower, for example, consciously thinking of the day ahead only to stop and wonder if I had washed my hair or not. I've probably washed my hair twice on many occasions. I would submit that our subconscious activities are based on preconditioned responses – "rule-based" routines or algorithms developed through repetition as we'll explore in the next section, and like in our software analogy, are activated and run in the "background" without our conscious awareness.

I would conjecture that our brain's structure of neighborhoods of connected neurons – the small-world interconnection scheme discussed previously – contributes to this phenomenon. Ornstein[18], for example, introduces the concept of a "squadron of simpletons" that carry out unconscious tasks and feed information to our conscious minds.

I like to think of this as like a hierarchy within a large organization. As the CEO of a large company, for example, you do things like make strategic decisions, set a direction, develop a culture. But you likely don't turn a wrench on the factory floor. More likely, you have multiple levels of managers in an organizational structure who interpret and oversee the work of carrying out your strategic direction. And these layers of managers also interpret lower-level data and provide you with the information you use to make decisions.

So it is with your brain. You are the CEO of your body and the thoughts and actions that it

53

performs. But, like the CEO of a company, much of your information comes from others in your organizational hierarchy. And, like the object models in our computing analogy, our brains produce models of the external world (and internal world, for example, in the case of dreams) and present them to our conscious selves. Our brains are multitasking, model-building, biological computers that feed information to our conscious selves like a conference room with the leaders of all the systems providing their interpretation of their data to put together a model for the conscious observer – the CEO, the self.

Every individual has different "voices" in their head – "their conference room". I, somewhat comically for example, have a DJ in my head who insists on playing songs or even commercial jingles that distract my concentration. I also "hear" the voice of my mother and my father, a frightened little boy and a wise old man, and a collection of friends and relatives who are residents in my memory. My brain has constructed models of all of them. We are all vulnerable to the influence of the residents in our brains, and to the potential to make sound or regretful decisions based on those influences. In my experience, however, there is one voice that is unique – the "I", the observer, the decision-maker, the CEO – who is ultimately responsible for high-level direction and who can overrule all the others.

Hofstadter[19] would likely disagree with the concept of an "observer" or decision maker. He proposed a simple model of consciousness consisting of small magnetic balls moving on a frictionless billiard table – a "careenium". The fact that the balls are magnetic means that the balls will form clusters (simmballs) that move and interact with each other and with the boundaries of the billiard table. Then by allowing the boundaries of the table to be flexible, and therefore influenced by external agents, the movement of the balls and clusters will display "memory" of the events. In this metaphor, the dance of simmballs in the careenium is like the dance of symbols in our brains. And, according to Hofstadter, it is the dance of symbols in our brains that *is* consciousness. As an interesting aside, by extrapolation of this metaphor the universe itself would possess consciousness. As a physicist, I am somewhat prone to reductionism and might be swayed by this description into thinking that consciousness and the universe are deterministic. I'll explore this further in the epilogue.

Hofstadter's metaphor is similar to the metaphor I offered above of the conference room with a collection of leaders offering their interpretation of their data. The simmballs bring their "interpretation" of external influences into the careenium. However, I see at least two basic differences that could be viewed as evolution from the simmballs in the careenium.

First, I see "thoughts" arising from the leaders in the conference room as interacting object models generated from a hierarchy of small computers (neural networks) much like Ornstein's squadron of simpletons. Second, and more importantly, I believe there is a goal-oriented control function – the ability to influence the pattern of dancing symbols or even slow them to a stop – as seen, for example, through the experience of meditation. I believe "thinking" is a directed flow of associations – symbols, thoughts, object models – with some goal. This is very similar to the attention schema described by Graziano, and provides us with the ability to model and predict the behavior of others – an evolutionary advantage that has been key to our survival.

So in my view, "thoughts" are expressed through all the residents in our heads – the seemingly constant updating of object models and construction of stories triggered by new sense data or revised or revisited connections. "Thinking", on the other hand, is a directed flow of thoughts. In the case of meditation, the objective is to stop the chatter, narration, and commentary that we all experience internally.

In "The Gradual Awakening"[20] for example, Steven Levine describes this process as first viewing the chain of thoughts as a movie and gradually stopping it. Eckhart Tolle, is his work "The Power of Now",[21] asks "I wonder what my next thought will be" and visualizes this process as waiting outside a mouse's hole for its appearance. Although I would not profess to have achieved any great level of meditation, these works have helped me to identify the constant flow of thoughts for what they are – my brain doing its thing based on evolution and a lifetime of experiences.

The two-computer model

To explore these concepts further, let's consider a simple two-computer model as illustrated in Figure 2.

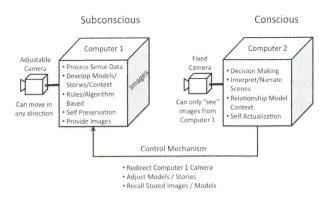

Figure 2

Computer 1 represents our subconscious brain, and could in fact be multiple computers as our subconscious brain is multitasking. In addition to maintaining the operation of the body, it's primary functions are to process sense data and develop object models – including comparing the data with other models in our library to build a story of how the new data "fits" within our existing base. It also "translates" our high-level vision into action – the "compiler". Computer 1's operations are "rules-based" or algorithm-based. An algorithm is optimized to some definition of success. In our case, the primary goal of Computer 1 is self preservation, which shapes the stories and object models it produces. Attached to Computer 1 is a camera that can move in any direction and takes in raw data to be processed, and is representative of our sense-data-collecting capabilities. Finally, upon completion of these tasks, Computer 1 presents images, based on it's processing, on a screen for viewing by Computer 2.

Computer 2 represents our conscious mind. It's primary operations are higher-level decision making, interpreting and narrating the scenes, and providing higher-level relationship-model context. The primary motivation of Computer 2 is self actualization – seeking to become something more. A key point is that Computer 2 only "sees" the external world through the models produced by Computer 1, but Computer 2 has a control mechanism over Computer 1. It can redirect Computer 1's camera, adjust the models and stories, and recall previously stored images and models. It can override the "instincts" of Computer 1.

Consequences of the two-computer model

The first consequence, as I just eluded to, is that our conscious minds only view the external universe through the lens of our subconscious brain and all it's preconditioned biases. The second is that we have a "loop" in our subconscious-conscious brain-mind system. In fact, if we cover Computer 1's camera – effectively close our eyes, remove all external sense data – we are performing a looping operation in which the output of the previous iteration provides the input for the next.

I'll return momentarily to the first consequence, but would like to first talk about the recursive, looping, nature of our subconscious-conscious system.

In the Introduction I mentioned that Hofstadter introduced the concept of a "strange loop" as a key to consciousness – a level-crossing feedback mechanism, Escher's Drawing Hands, a dynamical system in which the input of the next iteration is the output of the last. I claim that this is in part the interplay of our subconscious neural network, object-model programmer and our conscious observer, interpreter, narrator viewing the screen and directing the next action. This interplay of conscious / subconscious further reminds me of the thought experiments (Gedankenexperiment) popularized by Einstein[22]. The ability for us to learn through deductive reasoning versus new experiences requires reassembly of prior thoughts – knowledge – into something new – an internal, recursive process.

In the study of recursive dynamical systems, it has been shown that even deterministic systems can give rise to chaotic behavior and fractals.[23] The recursive iteration of some simple mathematical models can lead to very rich structures – e.g., chaos and fractals – that are found as well in nature.[24] I would conjecture that this might provide a mechanism for free will, creativity, and intuition – in addition to consciousness itself.

Now, reductionists might claim that the brain is composed of subatomic particles, and can therefore be understood at that level. Although that premise is of course true, the fact is that the patterns of neurons activating in the brain is dynamic and has a rich structure of its own. Like a computer producing fractal images based on the iteration of a simple function, the brain can produce activation patterns that are not predictable based on the structure of the brain alone.

We also discussed in the introduction Christof Koch's work advocating that causality is a key ingredient for consciousness. In the two-computer model above, our conscious mind has a causal impact on our subconscious in a recursive manner.

Finally, in Graziano's work the concept of attention, or an *attention schema,* was postulated to be a significant factor in the development of consciousness. The two-computer model provides for the concept of attention via the control mechanism.

I'm not implying here that a model like the two-computer model above would produce consciousness, but rather that it makes a useful description or metaphor of how we *experience* consciousness – how we think – and incorporates key elements of other authors. I'll revisit the two-computer model throughout the remainder of this work as a means of illustrating how our brain-mind system functions in different scenarios.

I am authoring, performing in, narrating, and viewing the movie in my head.

Now returning to the first consequence, the fact that our conscious mind only "sees" through the lens of our subconscious brain is necessarily a source of bias, but also the source of our intuition. It means that we view the world through conditioned responses that have been "learned" from birth or even hard wired from our evolutionary history – biased by the limitations of our experiences, our models, our metaphors. In short, our thinking, reasoning, and decision-making are based on a limited view of reality. In the study of inferential statistics, we learn that inferring conclusions from a biased sample is fraught with problems. Our subconscious brain is constantly processing information – for example, picking up queues from sense data and determining what needs to be fed to our conscious mind for more complex decision making.

There have been numerous studies in the field of behavioral economics,[25] that imply a "two-system" brain much like the two-computer model above. Very basically, those studies describe a "fast brain" or "automatic system" that operates at what I refer to as a subconscious level, and a "slow brain" or "reflective system" that operates at a conscious level. And, as I've also indicated above, those studies suggest bias in the fast system (our Computer 1). They in fact detail a list of biases – many of which may have evolutionary roots.

I'm not pointing at our "unconscious bias" as a fatal flaw, but rather an opportunity to become aware, learn, understand, and apply compassion to ourselves and others. It is an opportunity for societal awareness and improvement. Our evolutionary survival conditioning has taught us to fear differences. Fast forward to today and we arrive at the "tribal" segregation we see, for example, in politics, race, and national origin.

How does empathy fit in the model of ourselves and others? You are like me – I feel pain, therefore you feel pain. I value you because I value me. If I don't see you (my model of you) as like me, or if I don't value myself (and things like me) then I don't value you.

The worst things that happen in the world come from one human being seeing another human being as less than human.

How we learn

Before you can learn, you must first admit you don't already know.

The "learning" of a neural network in computing basically means that through repeated exposure to a data set, coupled with an error-minimization scheme, a response to future exposure becomes predictable.

In the case of human learning, I would expand this process to include the notion of "neural natural selection". What I mean by this is that our learning is continuous and occurs by introducing new information – sense data or thoughts (e.g., thought experiments, introspection, or reasoning) – into our system of models and if it survives by comparison with our existing knowledge or belief system, it forms new knowledge or belief. Our brains provide the environment for the "natural selection" of new information.

It now occurs to me that I need to say something about what I mean by knowledge and belief. OK, here goes: *Knowledge refers to the logical, coherent, evidence-based connection of a collection of information bits.* Further, when I say *belief* what I mean is that I'm lacking some aspect of my knowledge statement: *Belief refers to the connection of information bits based in whole or in part on supposition or conjecture – our brains "fill in" missing bits of information.* Philosophers have contemplated these questions for quite some time,[26] so I would only offer these statements as "good enough" for our purposes.

I find the distinction between knowledge and belief to be particularly important because we frequently operate, and make decisions and judgments, based on beliefs that are generated from our limited exposure – like inferential statistics based on a biased sample. The key word here is bias. *Beliefs require us to insert something from our internal reasoning based on our experience.* Beliefs are therefore biased by definition. The process of forming a belief is recursive – a conversation with ourselves – and, I believe, this process is linked to consciousness. Beliefs form an important part of our self model. They represent extrapolation from knowledge based on our subjective experience and reasoning.

Learning in our neural-network computing example occurs by adjusting weight factors. Learning in our brains is essentially accomplished in the same way – by altering our weight factors or synapses. Changing weight factors or synapse strengths allows us to change the functional or logic architecture of our brains – like changing the AND and OR gates we saw in the previous section. We can store information or relate bits of information to provide context. We can even "reprogram" our thinking, for example, by changing our object models via our weight factors. Learning can be achieved through new experiences – sense data processed – or through derivative processes – like thought experiments, deductive or inductive reasoning.

One of the challenges to learning, that we'll explore more shortly, is related to the bias in our brain-mind system – namely we have to be willing (consciously and subconsciously) to accept new information that may be contrary to our current models. We are attached, through repetitive reinforcement, to the models we've built – they provide us familiarity, comfort, and security. Repeated exposure to the same information reinforces connections – strengthening weight factors – that become difficult to overcome. Hence my statement, *before you can learn, you must first admit you don't already know.*

As in the previous section, I'll begin our discussion of learning with some computing examples, and then work by analogy to discuss how *we* learn. I'll then proceed to consider some of the challenges of how we learn.

Neural network revisited

So let's again consider a neural network consisting of nodes and weight factors. These networks usually contain multiple *layers* of nodes. The more layers of nodes, the "deeper" the learning – the number and variation of patterns increases with the number of layers. The network learns through training. Input data sets are provided with a known or expected output. For each data set, the actual output is compared to the expected output and an error is calculated. An error minimization scheme is employed, and a correction is calculated and applied to each weight factor. This process is repeated for each training data set until an acceptable level of accuracy is achieved. The network *learns* from its errors – learning from trial and error.

One of the things I find interesting about neural networks is that, having completed training, each subsequent stimulus is represented in the network by a pattern of nodes activating based on the now established weight factors – much like the neurons and synapses activating in our brains when we take in sense data. The pattern of nodes activated by an external stimulus acts as a *metaphor* for that stimulus. Additionally, each layer in a neural network provides an "interpretation" of the information provided by the previous layer (or original data) to the subsequent layer – like a hierarchy of information management, each layer only "sees" the output of the previous layer. So a neural network effectively contains a set of metaphors (patterns of nodes activating based on a set of weight factors) for external stimulus, and is subjective based on things like the weight factors, activation functions, error minimization algorithm, and number of layers used.

Early development

Let's now consider how this operates in us. From an evolutionary standpoint, learning and memory allow our nervous systems to adapt to the environment to optimize behavior. At the most fundamental level, learning is a process by which experience (i.e., subjective experience) changes an organism's responses. Infants, for example, are born with some level of knowledge – as a minimum, how to maintain the operation of their vital bodily functions or homeostasis. From there, early learning is trial and error – much like our neural network example – as they adapt to their environment. Even as they begin to learn language, a child will look at an object and utter a word (label) and as they are corrected or congratulated they learn – their weight factors or synapses are adjusting.

Now, since children don't immediately have a large pre-existing knowledge or belief system, they are not prone to a significant bias toward new information – they are "impressionable", their weight factors are not strongly reinforced by repetition. This allows them to absorb new information very quickly, and to develop their knowledge and belief systems. It is also, however, a critical period of time – their "formative years" – that will shape them for a lifetime. If, for example, they are treated with compassion and respect, and it is in turn expected of them, they will carry the belief that this is acceptable behavior. Their weight factors will reflect it, and it will be a "positive bias" in their accumulation of knowledge and belief. If, on the other hand, they are treated poorly (or for example exposed to violence and anger) this too will become their norm and all subsequent information will be filtered through this lens. *We are all the product of our experiences, and our early experiences form the filter for all future exposure.*

I would further argue that infants do not possess a significant level of consciousness from birth, but rather that consciousness develops with the increase of recursive thought processes – self awareness and the feeling of being alive. They also, in the process, develop the feedback and control mechanism illustrated in the two-computer model of Figure 2. As somewhat of an aside, I would argue that animals as well possess some level of consciousness. One need only observe crows, for example, in their family units to see, not only their self awareness, but their caring for members of their families.

Beyond trial and error

Learning can also occur by means of internal "thought" activities. Through a process of reconstruction, humans—and perhaps a few other animals—can use their learning operations to store, retrieve, and visualize previously stored memories. Humans have the capacity to reactivate neural actions that occurred in response to an earlier original stimulus – like the pattern of nodes activating in our neural network. I see this process of reconstruction as a fundamental difference between machine learning through trial and error, and human learning through recursive relational or associative model refinement.

Discoveries in physics, for example, frequently begin with a hypothesis. It may even start with asking ourselves "what if what we currently believe to be true is wrong – what other possibilities might there be." By opening our minds to possibilities and allowing free association of thoughts – 'brainstorming" – new ideas and models can form. This is an internal process of discovery and learning that can lead to wonderful new ideas, but unfortunately can also, through rumination and anxiety, lead to the creation of fictional worlds or psychological conditions. The process of creativity – creative thinking – can have more than one outcome.

Learning is both a conscious and subconscious activity. Our subconscious brain is learning and adjusting weight factors constantly – largely without our conscious awareness. We can, nonetheless, train our subconscious brain much like training a neural network in computing.

I like to play golf. However, the first time I tried to hit a golf ball the result was disappointing. I believe that's true for most unless you're somehow naturally gifted – i.e., born with a system of weight factors that naturally lends itself to striking a golf ball. I was told early on that I needed to hit something like ten thousand golf balls before I would become a "good" golfer – referring to "muscle memory". I'm sure most would agree that, although muscles may strengthen with repeated use, it's not our muscles that remember, but rather that we're training our subconscious brains – adjusting our weight factors – through repeated trial, error, and correction. Now I don't consciously adjust my weight factors directly, but I do recognize a good shot from a bad shot and "think about" a correction at a "macro" level. My belief is that this macro envisioning leads to corrections at a micro level via the hierarchy of *how we think* discussed previously. It is quite probable that visualization is an effective learning or conditioning tool as it serves to exercise the same neural patterns as the actual occurrence.

Motivation and challenges

So what motivates us to learn? As I mentioned previously, I believe the fundamental motives are self preservation and self actualization. According to me, this applies to learning as well. Self actualization in this regard is largely self evident – we can improve ourselves by learning. I want to become a better golfer, so I "practice" hitting golf balls in different ways under different conditions to continue to hone my weight factors. I was curious about the nature of reality, so I studied theoretical physics. By the way, although curiosity and wonder arguably have evolved for self preservation, I would place the higher-level curiosity and wonder referred to here under self actualization (desire) since it leads to advancement of understanding with no immediate consequence to my survival.

Learning as a means of preservation also seems obvious, but there are additional subconscious aspects that are worth exploring. If I feel uncertainty about the future, and as a result feel anxiety, I search (forage) for information that will relieve my anxiety and make me feel more secure. I forage for information that supports my beliefs. I believe this foraging for information is rooted in the foraging habits of our hunter-gatherer ancestors in their pursuit of food for survival. In the face of uncertainty and anxiety, we tend to "gather" and stockpile for security.

All animals must forage for food in order to meet their energetic needs, but doing so is energetically costly. Once again, natural selection has provided an efficient strategy to balance energy gain and energy consumption – often referred to as Marginal Value Theory.[27]

In simple terms, a marginal value refers to the change associated with the addition of one item – for example in economics marginal cost is the cost to produce one more item, marginal revenue is the revenue generated from the sale of one additional item, and marginal profit is the revenue minus the cost. With a little help from calculus,[28] we can show that profit is maximized when the marginal revenue equals the marginal cost. Intuitively, we might imagine that when the change in revenue generated from one additional item equals the change in cost, we've reached the maximum profit. Now, if we let revenue be the energy we gain from acquiring a "bit" of food and cost be the energy we expend to obtain that "bit" of food, then profit is the net gain of energy. Further, if we want to maximize our net energy gain (profit), then we look for the condition where the total gain of energy to acquire one additional bit of food (marginal revenue) is equal to the cost to acquire that bit of food (marginal cost).

We may actually want to start shopping for alternatives prior to reaching the point of maximum profit. A better goal in foraging might be to maximize the average profit of the items we obtain – sometimes referred to as the point of diminishing returns. That point is achieved when the average profit equals the marginal profit.[29] Beyond that point, the average profit is decreasing and we should start looking for alternatives.

Let's consider the example of picking berries in a berry patch. The benefit is a berry, and every berry has the same value regardless of the time required to acquire it – that is, the average revenue is constant. The cost is the time required to find a berry (which is directly related to the energy used). Initially the berries are easy to find, but eventually it takes more and more time. When the time required to find one more berry is equal to the average time, it's a signal to look toward another patch.

Fast forward to today, and we have brought this foraging behavior to our search for information. We "pick" information bits from a source until we reach diminishing returns (support of our beliefs) then we switch to another source. Our lives today are rich in the abundance of information with things like television, the internet, and social media. However, as opposed to the past where information was somewhat more "regulated" – for example, newspapers or printed books contained in libraries, or of more limited distribution like word-of-mouth – today "information", regardless of value or fact, can be posted by anyone.

Let's suppose, for example, the events around me have given me a feeling of uncertainty and anxiety. I go foraging for information – let's say via the internet, which seems to be the most available source of information. But, because of the bias I've developed over time in my brain's library of models, I am subconsciously prone to accepting – and learning from – only information that serves to reinforce my existing bias. Further, volume and intensity of message can make false claims persuasive, especially when listeners get all their information from like-minded sources. And it gets worse from there. Our attention is directed and cultivated for profit. In order to keep us "picking berries" from a specific patch (i.e., web page) information is presented to us based on our interests. The use of "cookies", for example, to track our interest and "feed" us information bits to cultivate our "clicks".

This is the place of things like conspiracy theories, prejudice, and reinforcement of our tribal segregation. We seek simple explanations based on our existing bias, and will discard any information that is contrary – and I would argue much of this occurs subconsciously. I am learning out of fear (survival), and accepting only information that aligns with my model of reality – my "comfort zone" – and information providers, seeking to shape our choices, use this fact.

Disinformation or conspiracy theories that offer simple explanations for otherwise random events help restore a sense of control or comfort. We use cognitive shortcuts – largely subconscious "rules-of-thumb" – to make decisions faster and to determine what to believe. And when we're experiencing anxiety or a sense of disorder, we crave conclusions or closure and we become even more prone to those cognitive shortcuts.

Now recall in our discussion of the two-computer model, the role of Computer 1, or subconscious brain or fast brain, is self preservation. I would contend that the "self" in this context is more than the physical self. It includes our belief system or our system of models and metaphors. Our subconscious Computer 1 seeks support and preservation for our psychological self. And our conscious mind is the recipient of the models produced by our subconscious brain.

I'm convinced that confronting these challenges with facts will not change minds that are ingrained in their beliefs. It occurs to me that we have to begin by addressing the source of the fear and the methods used to exploit those fears. We'll explore this more in the next section, but it is important to note here that I've used the word "facts". Like my previous distinction between knowledge and belief, we also need to distinguish facts from opinions. For example, when I say "it's cold outside", that's an opinion. When I say "it's twenty degrees outside", that's a fact.[30] All too often our learning is based on the opinions of others rather than independent facts.

One final thought on the challenges of learning in the presence of our experience bias, that may be an avenue for overcoming it, is this:

People learn more from discovery than they do from being told.

I believe more associations are formed in our brains in the process of discovery – more context, engagement, a feeling of achievement, an emotional tie to the information – than from simply being told. Learning occurs most rapidly, and we are generally happiest, when faced with moderately difficult challenges that we can overcome. Learning is not a purely intellectual activity but something embedded in our ability to accomplish tasks such as figuring out how to get to new places and deal with new people.

Using this concept as an approach to teaching arguably started with the "Socratic Method".[31] If we can create curiosity and encourage minds to become open to discovery, then learning becomes enjoyable and effortless.

Stories, in books and movies for example, provide us with opportunities to develop curiosity and channel it to identify with characters which help us learn empathy. Stories can be a useful tool to let us feel what others might experience. They can also be used, unfortunately, to "dehumanize" others making it easier to dismiss or even discriminate. Video games, for example, that engage players in violent behavior are contributing to this dynamic. It's difficult for me to believe that the experience of perpetrating violence in a "game" doesn't affect brain dynamics that ultimately have consequences in "real" life. Television shows and movies that make violence seem commonplace or somehow acceptable also contribute to "desensitizing" us.

Nevertheless, the more we can promote positive sources of learning – stories that help us identify with others, "see through their eyes", feel their joy and suffering – the more likely we are to challenge our own biases and learn empathy.

I am a white male, and was born and raised in the midwestern United States. And although I've lived in most sections of the country and traveled much of the world, I am still prone to seeing the world through my white, male, midwestern, United States lens. I frequently need to remind myself that my immediate perceptions are provided by that filter, and make every attempt I can to change my perspective to see that of others.

But I also learned compassion from my parents who stressed the importance of understanding the plight of others. I was an impressionable child during the civil rights movement and Vietnam war protests of the 1960s, and my parents provided perspective and context for those times that helped shape my perspective. I learned about things like prejudice, fairness, kindness, and compassion. Providing context to children for the world they're experiencing is important – particularly during their young impressionable years. I was fortunate to have parents who took the time to provide that context, and who provided me with diversity in my experiences. As children, we look to the people we know and trust to help shape our understanding. How we communicate matters – especially with children.

How we communicate

We measure ourselves based on our intentions – others measure us based on our actions.

Fundamentally, communication is a means for individual things to "connect" with one another in some way, or even to operate as a collective or en masse. As I mentioned in the introduction, communication is a necessary condition for the formation of multicellular entities, for the Neolithic Revolution, for the Industrial Revolution, and for the current age of electronic information. Earlier in human development, communication outside an immediate group was challenging. Now, the advent of the internet has allowed even relatively isolated individuals or groups to find a community – for better or worse. Communication has enabled us all to become part of the vast machine that is humanity.

You can feel it as you walk through a city. It may be as simple as strangers passing on the sidewalk exchanging a glance to navigate their passage, or maybe to provide a glimmer of recognition for someone we've passed before, or to trigger our "friend-or-foe" response mechanism.

Some of this occurs even without "eye contact" or conscious awareness.

It might also be a television commercial attempting to trigger an emotional response – fear, guilt, sexual attraction – to guide our attention toward their product or agenda. It might be a conversation with a loved one sitting in front of you who knows at a glance what you're thinking. Or it could be the conversation in your own head, or the voice you've assigned to me as you read the words on this page that I've written at some time in the past. We communicate through the clothes we wear, the house we live in, the car we drive, the way we walk, our speech mannerisms, and our words. There are many ways we send and receive signals.

In this section we'll focus on interpersonal communication (one-to-one or one-to-few) and mass communication (one-to-many or many-to-many) against the background of the previous sections. In particular, we'll consider how our thinking and learning, and our library of models and metaphors shape both our delivery and our reception of messages, and further how our subconscious intuition influences much of our lives. The goal being to continue to expose our bias, our vulnerability, and our humanness, and ultimately to encourage a direction shift toward a more compassionate society (or in Alex Trebek's words, "a kinder, gentler, society").

We'll visit the concepts of synchronous versus asynchronous, conscious versus subconscious (intuition), verbal versus non-verbal, literal meaning versus intent, and motivation and manipulation. And I would contend from the start that all communication is in some way manipulative. We communicate with the intent of causing something to happen or produce some result. What's important to understand is how we're being manipulated and why. I would confess that, more often than not, when I communicate *intentionally* with someone it's because I'm seeking connection.

Interpersonal communication

So let's begin by considering the mechanics of one-to-one, synchronous, face-to-face communication. Superficially, when I speak with someone, the process is to form a concept, encode the concept into words, and transmit the words. And the person with whom I am speaking will hear (receive) the words, decode the words, and produce a corresponding concept. However, this process of concept, encode, transmit, receive, decode, concept can have challenges at every step.

For example, the concepts I form are based on my individual experiences – my set of models and metaphors. Recall, in the introduction I mentioned that when I hear the word cat, I think of Sammie our chocolate-point Himalayan. You likely have a different image in your mind. Further, my ability to encode those concepts into words depends on my vocabulary and understanding of a language, and my transmission may include distracting or enhancing mannerisms – voice tones, facial expressions, or "body language". Similarly, on the receiving side, hearing and decoding the words depends on the attention and vocabulary of the listener. And in both cases our subconscious biases may enhance or inhibit our ability to transmit and receive. Finally, and most importantly, the real communication occurs when and if the decoded concept matches the intended concept, which depends on the listener's library of models and metaphors.

This is a tall order and depends not only on my listener and me having common metaphors or common experiences (more on this later), but also on the subconscious communication taking place through things like voice tone, facial expressions, eye contact, and body language – all the intuitive aspects of communication. In fact I may alter the words I'm using or my facial expressions and voice inflection depending on what I perceive of my listener's understanding based on their body language. And further, much of my adjustments and my listener's reactions may be quite subconscious and unknown to us both. We may even be surprised by the reactions we sense because we're unaware of our own actions. We may walk away from a conversation thinking "what just happened?".

So what's going on? Let's return briefly to the two-computer model (referring here to Fig 2 and surrounding text). Recall, our conscious mind (Computer 2) "sees" the world through the filter (models) of our subconscious brain (Computer 1). Computer 1 produces its models through a lifetime of conditioning (rules or algorithm-based) and adjusting of "weight factors" – our "learning" – and its primary motivation is "self" preservation. So the filter through which our conscious mind receives communication is biased, and is to a large extent shaped by our fears.

In the end, if we manage to achieve a match of concepts with someone, the connection is nothing short of amazing. We all want to be heard, to be understood, to feel that connection. When it happens, we feel less alone, we feel empathy, we identify with someone else and believe they identify with us.

In spite of the challenges, the exchange of ideas, matching of concepts, and achievement of understanding happens frequently. One example is comedy. A comedian uses common experiences to relate to an audience. By adding some nuance or "twist" of words or expression, a comedian forms a connection to our experiences in a way that we find humorous.

Common experiences need not occur at the same place and time to be "shared" or common. A common experience can be shared by two lives that never intersect. As a human, we all have bodily functions, we're all born and we all die, we all feel pain – both physical and emotional, we all eat and sleep, most of us wear clothes and brush our teeth with some regularity, maybe we have siblings or a spouse or children or pets. Maybe we've traveled to the same places, or eaten at the same restaurants, or worked in the same vocation. Maybe we've seen the same movies or read the same books. Stories are a way of creating common experiences and sharing alternate viewpoints, as is music or poetry or art.

If we didn't have common experiences or have familiarity with the nuances of a language, we might have difficulty reaching an understanding or even appreciating a particular joke.

I had the privilege of mentoring a young Japanese student. In writing her college entrance application, one of the things that she indicated as a notable experience was growing up between the United States and Japan with Japanese and Korean parents who sometimes spoke English. A point she made was that, as a result of her multi-lingual upbringing, there were some subtleties of both the English and Japanese languages that she didn't completely grasp. And in particular, sometimes jokes were lost on her due to those subtleties.

So in the process of concept, encode into language, transmit, receive, decode, and finally to concept, there are many ways, even mechanically, for communication to fail.

In some settings it might be easy to dismiss or marginalize someone whose experiences or grasp of a language are not the same as our own. We naturally enjoy the company of others with whom we relate. We're most comfortable with others "like us". Communication is easier. This tendency has the potential for the unfortunate consequence of encouraging us to self-segregate, and, taken to the extreme, to diminish or dehumanize others. This behavior underscores the importance of relating humanness. As we encounter barriers to communication, particularly based on differences of experiences (our set of models and metaphors), I believe it's important to "shift perspectives". That is, take the perspective of an independent observer. Be curious rather than judgmental, and remember our common humanity.

I was leading a small group of high-potential future executives on a three-month project to address a company concern. Early in the project, it was our practice to do a "norming" exercise where we talked about how we might best work together. Things like our most productive times of day, our aptitudes, or even our dislikes. One individual said to me "I will likely drive you crazy because I'm a non-linear thinker and communicator, and you're very linear." It occurred to me that this person was able to take the perspective of an independent observer and saw a difference between us that could've led to conflict. It was a valuable lesson, and one that I sometimes need to remind myself.

My wife Vicky and I joke about our grocery-shopping trips. If I go to the store to buy a gallon of milk, I will emerge from the store soon after I enter with precisely a gallon of milk. Vicky might emerge from the store after quite some time with a bag full of groceries that may or may not contain a gallon of milk. She has in some sense achieved more than I did as everything in her bag is useful, but she may have lost sight of the original goal. I, on the other hand, am hyper focused on the goal and may consequently miss opportunities. Another example is how we navigate. I navigate by consulting my mental map of street names. She navigates by landmarks. Neither of these is more or less correct. Our experiences and our resulting models provide conditioning that prescribes how we operate. What's important is recognizing and valuing those differences.

We'll revisit the concept of common experiences in our discussion of mass communication, but it leads me to question the possibility of a foundational set of experiences, and therefore a corresponding set of models and metaphors, that provide a basis for common understanding. I think we would all agree that the more background we have in common, the easier it is to communicate. The converse is almost certainly true as well. Recognizing this, without assigning fault when communication feels difficult, is a key step toward empathy.

Now, there are unfortunately cases where a person may want to communicate with the intent to deceive. I mentioned previously that I believe all communication is in some sense manipulative – intended to cause something to happen or produce a result. However, communicating with the intent to deceive occurs when words, actions, beliefs, and values are not aligned. The intent of deception is to promote a belief in the receiver that is not consistent with the actual belief of the transmitter. It could be as simple as altering a physical appearance, or more complex like leveraging a known fear or anxiety of a receiver to encourage them to adopt a belief that is advantageous to the transmitter.

Recall from our previous discussion on how we learn, my thoughts on beliefs are: *belief refers to the connection of information bits based in whole or in part on supposition or conjecture – our brains "fill in" missing bits of information.* If we're fed information bits that are presented as fact and are aligned with our fears or existing beliefs, we're prone to deception.

We learn some level of deceit as children. It comes to us as self preservation. If we fear a punishment, we create a narrative that promotes our innocence, and we subsequently build that narrative into our self model. We can, in fact, also deceive ourselves in this way. This is again Computer 1 at work protecting us and our system of models. My self model says I'm not a bad person; lying is bad; therefore I'm not lying.

In other cases, direct communication might be frowned upon, so indirect approaches may be used instead; like putting a "spin" on a comment or "sowing seeds of doubt" in order to create a belief that is aligned with our desire. This is Computer 2 working for some kind of gain. Self actualization can have a dark side too. Deceptive communication is rampant in politics and advertising, as we'll explore more in our next topic on mass communication. The key point is that communication occurs at many levels and has many subtleties.

As we move progressively from face-to-face, synchronous communication to remote synchronous, to remote asynchronous (e.g., recorded voice), to text, elements of communication are progressively lost – like voice tone or body language. An interesting point to me is that along with those lost elements of communication is a reduction in the potential for bias – particularly subconscious bias based on things like appearance or voice tone or speech mannerisms. If our judgement of a result was based solely on the result and not who produced it (like a "blind taste test"), would our judgement be different?

As you're reading this text, you're not likely reacting to my race or gender or appearance. You're reading these words with a voice created in your mind. You've created a model of me based only on the information I've provided. Now, in this book I've given you information about my race, gender, and cultural origins, but your model of me likely includes subconscious elements based on my writing style. But in a face-to-face interview that might be very different. Our subconscious bias provided by Computer 1 plays a key role in our reaction to others.

With some of the subtleties of communication in mind, we now turn to the topic of mass communication.

Mass communication

Mass communication begs the question why – why would someone, or a group of someones, want to communicate with a large number of others? I believe both of what I refer to as our primary motivations (self preservation and self actualization, or fear and desire) can be responsible. I open with this question because as we evaluate the messages we receive through the various channels of mass communication, it's important to understand the motivation – the real motivation. We're too often deceived or manipulated for someone else's gain. My goal is again to expose our vulnerability and our bias.

When I did research in physics and published results, I was communicating to a broad audience (well that was my hope anyway, although the theoretical physics audience isn't all that large). I would argue that my motivation was self actualization. My hope was to further the forefront of science. In writing this book, I am hoping to connect to a large audience. My goal is to promote a better, more compassionate, understanding of human nature. It's unlikely that I'll make much money from its publication, and I would again contend that my motivation is self actualization. In both cases I am hoping to improve something with little personal gain other than a good feeling for having contributed.

Things like stories, movies, art, and poetry give us (as transmitters) an opportunity to communicate to a large audience and also provide us (the receivers) with an opportunity to adopt a perspective change as I mentioned previously. We can, for example, assume the position of someone in a movie to gain their perspective. Or we can "experience" a different aspect of life as lived by another. These media forms can also help promote empathy and compassion by letting us feel the pain and joy of others. I consider these uses of media to be self actualizing. Someone or some group wants to encourage others to identify with a character or event or story – hopefully to promote understanding, compassion, and unity.

Throughout history, prior to the advent of movies and television, stories in the form of mythology and religion have served to provide common experiences to unite groups of people. Joseph Campbell, for example, wrote extensively on the "Power of Myth".[32] He described myth as serving four basic functions:

(1) The mystical / metaphysical – awakening and maintaining in individuals a sense of awe in, and gratitude for, the 'mystery of being'. According to Campbell, the mystery of life, what he called

transcendent reality, cannot be captured directly in words. Symbols and mythic metaphors, on the other hand, may offer insights into that reality.

(2) The cosmological – explaining the universe. For pre-modern societies, myth also functioned as a *proto-science*, offering explanations for the physical phenomena that surrounded and affected their lives, such as the change of seasons and the life cycles of animals and plants.

(3) The sociological – validate and support the existing social order. Throughout history societies have had to adopt and conform to a social order if they were to survive. Mythology reinforced that order by reflecting it in the stories, often describing how the order arrived from divine intervention.

(4) The pedagogical / psychological – guide individuals through the stages of life. As a person goes through life, many psychological challenges will be encountered. Myth may serve as a guide for successful passage through the stages of one's life.

These functions or themes form the bases for religion and are in fact present in many of our movies today, and much of our media. Movies, to some extent, serve as our modern mythology.

The same media forms or channels can unfortunately be used as a tool to sow fear and division. Self actualization and self preservation can as well have a negative side.

Consider a colony of prairie dogs for example. If one of them perceives a threat, he alerts the others. He is communicating to a broader group based on a perceived threat to the survival of the group. Sound familiar? How often do we see communication to a broad group that is based on a perceived threat to the survival of the group. Now in the case of the prairie dog, his aim is not likely deception. He's not likely looking to leverage the fear of the broader group for his own gain. Unfortunately in the case of politicians, businesses, and some news outlets, leveraging fear or desire is common.

By creating a scenario in which our way of life is somehow threatened, politicians or advertisers offer themselves or their products as a solution to alleviate our fear. They create the fear and then provide the solution. The recent trend toward nationalism is one example where a politician, like the prairie dog, has sounded the alert to a segment of the population that their way of life is threatened. But unlike the prairie dog, he contends that he alone holds the answer to protect them from the villains. And by donating to his campaign and giving him their vote, they will be saved. This is how autocrats gain power.

Likewise, desire can be leveraged to drive our behavior. How often do we see a television commercial that leads you to believe that if you had this car, these clothes, this cologne or perfume that you would somehow be like the person in the advertisement? I will never be taller, have a bronze complexion, and "washboard abs" no matter how much cologne I splash on.

So why are we so vulnerable to these tactics? I believe the answer can be illustrated again with our two-computer model. As noted previously, we use cognitive shortcuts – largely subconscious "rules-of-thumb" – to make decisions faster and to determine what to believe. And when we're experiencing anxiety or a sense of disorder, we crave conclusions or closure and we become even more prone to those cognitive shortcuts.

Conspiracy theories typically start with a conclusion that has some degree of plausibility. People then get attached to the conclusion and will search for any supporting evidence (recall our discussion on foraging) and dismiss any evidence to the contrary.

All lies and jests; Still a man hears what he wants to hear and disregards the rest. Paul Simon

In our discussion of the two-computer model, the role of Computer 1, or subconscious brain or fast brain, is self preservation. I would contend that the "self" in this context is more than the physical self. It includes our belief system or our system of models and metaphors. Our subconscious Computer 1 seeks support and preservation for our psychological self. And our conscious mind is the recipient of the models produced by our subconscious brain. The important point here is that if our system of models lacks sufficient breadth, we are vulnerable to disinformation that *appears* consistent with our existing models, and we are thereby vulnerable to deception. We continually incorporate the disinformation into our models and reinforce beliefs held in our Computer 1 brains. Differences in educational experiences across the country and the world contribute to this vulnerability and can lead to divisions based on the absorption of disinformation.

So if our system of models is threatened, our Computer 1 brain feeds our Computer 2 mind quick solutions. And if Computer 2 sees a way to improve our "self image" (self model), then maybe a new cologne or new car is in order.

Money, media, and politics have historically been the primary elements of the underlying system that dictates mass communication. With the advent of the internet and social media, however, it's possible for anyone to cultivate a following and espouse disinformation. There's a growing likelihood that in fact some of our information isn't coming from individuals at all, but rather from AI computer algorithms such as the text-generating language model ChatGPT.[33] When you enter a web search into your computer, the response is very likely coming from one of these algorithms, which are themselves prone to bias or even deception.

Media in general is driven by money and the pursuit of power. The typical news story, for example, of "man bites dog" will almost always be reported ahead of "dog bites man" due to the unusual nature of the story. Our attention is captured by something different or unusual, as is the case with conspiracy theories. Man bites dog is reporting the exception rather than the normal. This method is frequently used to imply that what is in fact an exception is actually wide spread. It grabs our attention and our attention has value. It is also well known that action, violence, and sex in film, television, and video games all trigger heightened attention. Our attention is directed or manipulated to sell items or advertising. So media is incentivized to grab and hold our attention with more and more unusual stories and sensationalism.

That brings us to one of the biggest challenges in mass communication: finding a trusted source for facts. There's evidently no requirement for "news" outlets to report facts or clearly distinguish between facts and opinions. And in many cases even the facts are reported with "spin" or slant intended to sway belief, create excitement, and capture our attention.

In my opinion, news should be a public service to inform and educate viewers about events. It should not be for profit. As many of our news programs have become profit conscious audience chasers, the material and reporting have become sensationalized and tailored to excite viewers. In some cases, "news" programs have even become political propaganda distributors. I find it interesting to look at who owns a given "news" outlet and what their motivation might be.

When you see stories in the news, and even more importantly in social media, you might stop and wonder why you are seeing this story, and consider whose attention (what segment of society) are they attempting to influence and why?

As more and more information floods our senses we rely more and more on our fast brain (Computer 1), but it's simultaneously becoming more and more important to engage our Computer 2 reasoning mind to discern what's occurring – what's fact, what's opinion, what's bias, what's deception, and how we are being manipulated. Again, when I say "it's cold outside",

106

that's an opinion. When I say "it's twenty degrees outside", that's a fact.

Reality is nothing more than an agreed to set of perceptions built upon past experiences.

So what can we do?

The path ahead

We exist temporarily through what we take, we live forever through what we give. Vernon Jordan

We've focused in the previous sections on how we think, learn, and communicate with the goal of better understanding our bias and our vulnerability; and to recognize that these attributes are by-and-large a result of our human nature, our environment, and our evolution. That doesn't excuse us from working to improve. Indeed, now that we better understand our nature, it's incumbent on us all to do more, and to do better. Become more aware of your subconscious bias and vulnerability represented by your "Computer 1", algorithm-based brain and become more conscious.

Be more. Be the artist, the physicist, the philosopher, the janitor, the mechanic, the teacher, the mother, the father, but be more. Be the person who promotes social justice; and racial, gender, educational, and economic equality. Be the person who steps up when others are afraid. Be the person who runs toward the fire no matter whose life it saves. Empathize, become more compassionate.

Our biological structure (hardware) has been conditioned and established for a long time based on the evolution of millions of years. But the patterns of symbols in our minds (software) may be evolving rapidly. I stated previously my belief that Natural Selection applies to everything – including our brain development. But it seems to me that we can guide or influence the evolution of our models. We can collectively learn.

Challenging the models that are ingrained in our brains requires examination of the mechanisms responsible. Competition for resources is one such evolutionary mechanism in brain development.[34] This competitive nature permeates our psyche and, in my opinion, contributes to the tribal rivalry on display across much of our society. Again, Natural Selection applies to everything.

Campbell pointed out how mythology (including religion) has historically had a key role in unifying people into cultural groups. However, coupled with our competitive nature, the unification of individuals into cultural groups and their segregation of others has led to religious, race, socioeconomic, and political conflicts that have existed for centuries.

In modern times, as there's been more movement away from traditional religions, somewhat of a void has been created for unifying ideals. There's also been, as a result, a desire by some to reestablish that "old time religion" and a trend toward fundamentalism.

To this point Campbell said: "On this immediate level of life and structure, myths offer life models. But the models have to be appropriate to the time in which you are living, and our time has changed so fast that what was proper fifty years ago is not proper today. The virtues of the past are the vices of today. And many of what were thought to be the vices of the past are the necessities of today. The moral order has to catch up with the moral necessities of actual life in time, here and now. And that is what we are not doing. The old-time religion belongs to another age, another people, another set of human values, another universe. By going back you throw yourself out of sync with history. Our kids lose their faith in the religions that were taught to them, and they go inside."[35]

So how do we fill the void and how do we evolve our models? I'm not advocating some type of new religion, but rather a framework that includes the four functions articulated by Campbell, because I believe those do have the potential, with time, to unify diverse cultural groups. But this framework must also incorporate economic incentives that drive behaviors in the right direction, and educational and legislative changes that promote social consciousness. It should also leverage, and evolve with, the rapid pace of technology. And as Maslow pointed out in his hierarchy of needs,[36] we need to relieve people of their fear, make basic necessities readily accessible, and help them with a purpose for their actualization.

This is a tall order and some may ask why even attempt this? Well, as I indicated in the introduction it appears we are at a tipping point. The path we're on has a reasonable likelihood of leading to the end of our species, and to stand idly by and wait for it to happen is simply unacceptable. Some might say I'm idealistic. To them I would say "I agree", but my expectation is simply to "plant seeds" that might one day bear fruit and affect a course shift.

My proposals are largely US-centric, as that is the majority of my familiarity, but I believe with little effort they can be extended elsewhere. And I would again stress, as I did in the prologue, this is simply one person's opinion and attempt to chart a course.

So the following is a collection of ideas – a framework – organized around five elements:

1. Scientific / Spiritual

2. Sociological

3. Economic

4. Educational

5. Legislative

I'll now discuss these in turn, then summarize.

Scientific / Spiritual

I've combined the first two categories advocated by Campbell into one because, as a physicist, I believe that awakening an individual's sense of awe in, and gratitude for, the "mystery of being", and explaining the universe can be aligned. It may seem somewhat provocative to combine science and spirituality into one area, but I have found the beauty of science and the boundaries of our scientific understanding to invite my spirituality.

I began studying physics as a quest for understanding. As I mentioned in the prologue, I consider myself a spiritual person, but not ascribing to any formal religion. I've been plagued throughout my life with the gnawing uncertainty of "being" and what it means. Physics provided me an avenue to ask questions and search for answers. And when I find myself at the limits of our current understanding, I have the opportunity to explore my spirituality. I have a deep appreciation for the beauty of our physical universe, but leave the door open for something more (more on this in the Epilogue).

Physics is descriptive of "how" things happen, but only answers "why" by employing more "fundamental" descriptions of "how". The point is that ultimately the question of why can only be answered in terms of one's own spirituality. The mysteries of the physical universe exposed through modern physics (like quantum field theory and general relativity) provide me with that sense of awe and gratitude described by Campbell, and leave ample room for spiritual inquiry. In my view our scientific and spiritual experiences are inextricably joined and must be reconciled.

I would make this charge to all scientists, philosophers, and religious leaders (and people in general for that matter): be clear on what you know, be open to what you don't, and be accepting of *beliefs* that are different than your own provided they advocate no harm to others. The hope for something more and the quest for meaning provides a necessary purpose for people.

For example, in his book "Man's search for meaning",[37] neurologist and psychiatrist Viktor Frankl credits his theories on meaning (Logotherapy) for helping him survive his holocaust experience. Simply put, Logotherapy is based on the belief that striving to find meaning in life is the primary, most powerful motivation in humans. I include this in what I refer to broadly as self-actualization.

I would ask scientists, philosophers, and religious leaders to unite around some basic principles.

Denounce things like violence, hate, segregation, and inequality; and embrace empathy and compassion. Take even more of a leadership role in helping the general population gain understanding and appreciation for the beauty and awe of being, both in our universe and within each of us. In practice, this might be world religious leaders, philosophers, and scientists forming an alliance and speaking publicly, visibly, on these topics. Utilize the technology of today to communicate with diverse populations.

Sociological

I begin this section by stating that I am by no means an expert on the subject of sociology, but am an observer of life focused on understanding patterns and proposing some ideas. I have also, once again, chosen to combine two of Campbell's functions because I believe the following thoughts pertain to both. To that end, my focus here is on social norms and how to instill more empathy and compassion in our norms, and how the resulting structure can help to support people throughout their lives.

There are laws established by governments that document societal norms. But there are also implied agreements or "norms" of acceptable behavior we have with our society – an implied contract of sorts. These norms are sometimes set or changed by leaders. For example, a company leader might decide that suits are no longer necessary on Fridays and casual dress is OK. Or norms may be ingrained in a religious practice or tradition like head coverings. In other cases, there might be long-established norms that have grown out of efficiency, like in the case of driving. There is also a level of "politeness" (or lack of) that varies culturally as we travel from place to place.

Vicky and I enjoy international travel, and were fortunate enough to take a trip to Japan. We were taken by the politeness of the culture. For example, we were traveling by train from Tokyo to Kyoto. A cell phone rang and the owner of the phone, a younger gentleman, quickly moved to the space between compartments so as not to disturb the other passengers. In another observation, we noticed it was common for everyone on an escalator to stand to one side so that others might pass. The politeness that seems common in Japan appears largely absent in the "me-first" culture in the US.

As I mentioned in the introduction, technology is driving our culture more and more. The structure and roles of our society are changing as technology evolves. The jobs of yesterday, for example, are not the same today, and those of today will likely not be the same tomorrow. Nor are the ways we travel, or drive (how will self-driving car algorithms and AI incorporate politeness versus aggression), or the way we communicate. The world has become more "connected" with technological advances.

As well as potentially helping norms evolve in a positive sense, mass communication via social networks is also providing the means for more or less anonymous commentary on people and topics, which can consequently erode acceptable norms of behavior. This relative anonymity allows people to distance themselves from the impact of their actions. It has a dehumanizing effect. I would submit that, for most, standing in front of someone and witnessing the pain that is caused by one's actions – one human being to another – would alter their deeds.

This is unfortunately not always the case. Christopher Browning, in his book "Ordinary Men",[38] described how in World War II the systematic dehumanization of Jews and the creation of a fictional moral imperative (a norm based on lies), led to "ordinary men" carrying out atrocities.

Some of these norms, I believe, are the result of "herd mentality" or fear of missing out (FOMO), or in short, simply fear. From an evolutionary standpoint, being separated from the "herd" is dangerous. So our Computer 1 brain feeds us fear messages to help us stay in the pack. But what if the herd is moving in the wrong direction – say off a cliff? This is how participants in a mob or protest later, upon conscious reflection, come to regret their actions. They come "face-to-face" with the impact of their deeds.

There are times throughout history in which a level of social anxiety has led to an abandonment of established norms. I believe this is often due to economic stratification – whether perceived or real. This condition is amplified today by rapidly changing technology. There are, and will continue to be, people who are left behind and missing the benefits of change. This, at times, leads to social uprising and can be leveraged by leaders seeking to increase their following based on fear and anger. I've told my MBA students to be aware that the ground beneath their feet is constantly moving and they need to be constantly reinventing themselves to adapt.

So the questions are how do we shape a culture and the associated norms? How do we "recondition" our Computer 1 brains? How do we carry out a "systematic humanization" to promote greater empathy and compassion?

In my opinion the answer lies in understanding the influences, and using them to reshape our thinking. It starts with things like movies, television, leaders (political and religious), and literally the people who refer to themselves as influencers. But we also have to embed norms in our institutions – schools, military service, social programs. We need a clear set of common experiences and corresponding models and metaphors to provide a basis for empathy – an enduring, global, cultural story.

I'm not implying here that there is one single story, but rather a collection of stories about people and their hardships, their successes, their love, and their pain. These would be stories about being human told from the perspective of the subject person and how the events of their lives affected them. They should include historical information and facts about our journey as humans – how far we've come and how far we have to go, history from the perspective of individuals experiencing it.

I'm a big fan of Wikipedia. It serves as a source of publicly-refereed material. It represents knowledge as a collective agreement contained in a set of articles. I would propose to the leaders of endeavors like Wikipedia, Public Broadcasting, the Library of Congress, and film and television productions to bring more stories from people of diverse backgrounds told from the perspective of the subject person with the goal of promoting empathy. We need to do more to embed these stories in our educational systems at all levels. And I would appeal to influencers to help promote these stories.

I would also propose a paid social program (as opposed to, or expansion of, volunteer programs like AmeriCorps) to employ people to perform public-service tasks. This would serve multiple purposes. First, it would provide a starting point and opportunity for young people entering the workforce. Second, it would provide a "safety net" for people who are out of work and may serve as an alternative to, or an addition to, unemployment. Finally, and most importantly, a program like this can provide a basis for common experiences that might increase empathy.

Now, there are certainly those who would argue that these are "socialist" ideas. The topic of this section is, after all, "sociological". It is often easier to reject ideas by labeling them with something that is a perceived threat. I am a big fan of capitalism. I believe, for example, that the reward of innovation provides a great incentive for the investment in research and development. I also believe, however, that providing basic necessities for a society, and some social safety nets, can further drive innovation and productivity. More on this in the sections that follow.

Nature does not equally distribute opportunities.

Economic

A simple economic axiom is that social programs require funding. And the funding must come from a source that has – you guessed it – funds. Why should those on the positive side of the ledger want to change? Why not – fear. Read it off – prosperous, educated, males (in the United States white) wanting to maintain a dominant role in society. And fearing that by giving opportunity to less privileged groups, their way of life is somehow threatened. This is the call of the prairie dog, and it is used to mobilize even the less fortunate and less educated to act based on this fear.

I am a prosperous, educated, white male and I don't feel threatened by providing opportunities for those less fortunate. Obviously my statement above doesn't apply to all, but I believe the sentiment is real. Maybe I'm "woke" (another label used to segregate and marginalize), but I prefer to think of it as being aware of the fear created by my Computer 1 brain versus the compassion of my Computer 2 mind.

As I mentioned previously, in my simplistic view, economics is the study of incentives and behaviors. We must therefore provide some incentives for those more fortunate to help create opportunities for those less fortunate. And from the start, I would rule out "trickle-down economics" as a model because it fails to recognize the greed of the people along the path to the bottom. The rich get richer and the poor get poorer. On the other hand, one of the primary objections to government programs is lack of visibility, control, and accountability and consequently waste.

So what incentives can be offered to those who have more to provide more for those who have less? And secondly, how do we prevent waste?

I'd like to begin with the second question first. Organizationally, large social programs must be federal-government sponsored. I would suggest, however, that a clear mission statement be established along with annual statements of budget and overhead cost versus benefit delivered, and that the program is overseen by a board made up of industry leaders. The government is essentially a nonprofit. So the measure of success should be overhead cost versus benefit delivered, and the transparency to, and management by, an industry board should alleviate any concerns of waste.

Now to the first question. Rather than a tax, I would begin with a voluntary, tax-deductible, charitable contribution made directly to the program (rather than a general bucket of discretionary spend). The psychological effect here is that taxes are seen as a "takeaway" whereas a charitable contribution is seen as generous giving. These contributions could in fact be made visible – a kind of "bragging right" for the wealthiest among us to support the betterment of society. The incentive is really the improved image and legacy of the contributors.

Educational

I believe, fundamentally, the answer to the question of how to increase the level of compassion and empathy in our society is education. Unfortunately what stands in the way is again fear. There is a segment of our society that believes, by having empathy and compassion for all people, they will somehow have to sacrifice their place. I believe it is again related to the competitive nature of our brain evolution that is pervasive in everything we do. Our Computer 1 brain is feeding us messages to sustain our place in the "social order". Overcoming this means offering reassurance, like the social safety nets mentioned in the previous sections, and helping people to become more aware of their Computer 1 brains.

Early brain development (wiring) is based on environmental conditions that thereby shape future learning, development, and understanding. Establishing compassion and empathy needs to start early, and needs to be reinforced at every level of education.

Vicky is an elementary school teacher and librarian. I've had an opportunity through her experiences to see the curriculum, the successes, and challenges of early childhood education. She was once involved with a program called Roots of Empathy.[39] Their mission is to build caring, peaceful and civil societies through the development of empathy in children and adults. They believe people need imagination and empathy to be able to identify and solve society's problems, and that empathy is foundational to helping children navigate relationships, form connections and be inclusive of others. They work toward achieving this mission through outreach to schools (training and curriculum) and by inviting community families into classrooms to demonstrate the power of a secure attachment relationship between infant and parent.

Vicky's experience with the program was positive. The children, particularly in smaller classroom settings, were engaged and responsive. I believe programs like Roots of Empathy are essential and should be expanded to all early childhood education. One of the challenges is how to fit such programs into an already overburdened curriculum. There has to be a prioritization scheme.

A prioritization scheme must start by asking the questions:

• What is the mission of K-12 education?

• What is the mission of post high school education?

I believe the answer to the first question is to prepare young people for life as adults. K-12 education should, therefore, be focused on both socialization and critical thinking, and for early learning it should focus heavily on socialization. It appears, however, that the current focus of curriculum is more about critical thinking, and socialization is simply assumed to occur through the exposure to other students.

What I mean by socialization here is of course empathy, compassion, and interpersonal skills; but also sociology and history – honest history, the facts, what actually happened. There have been efforts to "rewrite" history when the facts are uncomfortable. The ongoing debate on racial and gender inequities are cases in point. These lessons should be taught, not to cause guilt for what has happened, but to ensure it never happens again.

It seems to me that by investing an equal amount of time on socialization as critical thinking skills in our school systems many of the social and workplace challenges we see today could be greatly reduced or even eliminated. This increased focus would require smaller class sizes to allow greater attention to be applied, and the reduction in time devoted to other subjects. In short, we need socialization to be a priority in order to create a better society.

The mission of post high school education should be to provide the skills required for the future sustainment of our society and to further the forefront of knowledge. I believe in free education, but with compulsory courses in sociology. The goal being not only to increase the education level in total, but also to foster cross-cultural exposure, and promote improvement in societal norms.

I spent eight years in college, earning a B.S., M.S., and Ph.D.; and taught both undergraduate and graduate courses in both physics and business. The college environment is competitive and stressful for students, and forces them to quickly become narrowly focused in their chosen field of study. This can have the tendency to cause an inward focus and reduce empathy and compassion. At least one compulsory course in sociology might aid in promoting understanding, and thereby empathy and compassion.

People are an investment. I've payed more in taxes than I've ever received, and I'm happy to pay more if it leads to a more knowledgeable and compassionate society.

Legislative

I should preface the following with some context. Early in my life I saw via television the Cuban missile crisis, the assassination of John Kennedy, the assassination of Martin Luther King, the assassination of Robert Kennedy, the impeachment and resignation of Richard Nixon, the fall of the Soviet Union, Tiananmen Square, the Viet Nam war, two Iraq wars, multiple Afghanistan wars, the Ukraine war, and numerous others. I've been writing this book during the period of the global Covid-19 pandemic.

There seems now to be a plague of political stunts and buffoonery here in the United States that I can't recall seeing previously in my life; including the undermining of institutions that maintain order in our society, and arguably an attempted coup with the support of many right-wing politicians. The politicization of a pandemic – political leaders publicly mocking science, precautions, and life-saving vaccinations – for the sake of exciting a malinformed voting base, is in the least immoral and in my opinion criminal.

People have died needlessly because of a group of politicians' egos and their desire for power. Obviously vaccinations and mask wearing won't stop 100% of virus transmissions. But they are painless precautions and if they prevented even one death – maybe your mother, father, wife, or child – then it was worth it.

If leaders can't find a way to publicly denounce violence and hate, and stop trying to "spin" every event to their own advantage, then it's difficult for me to imagine how they can call themselves leaders. And we, in the general population, need to hold them accountable.

Now, with that as context, let's ask the questions:

• What is the role of legislation?

• What should we expect of legislators?

My goal here is not to attempt a course on government, but rather to promote a few simple principles that might affect some improvement, and I again state, as I have previously, that I am not an expert on this topic. Here's the simplistic explanation: the legislative branch writes laws, the judicial branch interprets laws, and the executive branch enforces laws. We've all likely heard this in our high school civics class. But what is the goal or role of legislation?

In my opinion the role of legislation should be to *ensure order, ensure security, and ensure rights for every individual – all people equally.* We probably all agree on the first three statements. Where we run into trouble is when your rights collide with mine – every individual and all equally.

It was only one hundred years ago (1920) that women gained the right to vote in the US. The Fifteenth Amendment (ratified in 1870) extended voting rights to *men* of all races. However, this amendment did not really help black Americans because state constitutions and laws, poll taxes, literacy tests, and outright intimidation still made it difficult or impossible for them to vote. Black Americans were not really given voting rights until 1965. It seems very unlikely that in less than one hundred years (in our white male dominant society) we have achieved all the legislative changes needed to ensure order, ensure security, and ensure rights for every individual – all people equally. One need only spend time with women and people of color, and be open to hearing their stories – empathize, to understand that there's still work to do.

So what should we expect of legislators? Simply, represent all people equally – not just the donors who contributed to your campaign, or the people who voted for you, but all people. Being a legislator should be a noble and humble cause, not a self-serving power trip. It is an opportunity to serve others and to be a leader. Do the right thing for the right reasons regardless of what it might mean for your career.

In a previous book,[40] I defined leadership as: *Leadership is the ability to bring out the best in others (maybe more than they knew they had) to achieve a goal or objective.* The goal in this case, again, should be *ensure order, ensure security, and ensure rights for every individual – all people equally.* I would ask legislators to consider your legacy and take to heart the Vernon Jordan quote: "We exist temporarily through what we take, we live forever through what we give."

Summary

The thoughts above are an effort to provide some actionable ideas on a path to improvement. They are likely simplistic and naive. But maybe simplistic is what's required. I believe that at times the solutions offered to social problems are made too complicated to be effective, or worse are destroyed by their own girth or abandoned before they start. My message here is to do something. Even small steps in the right direction can have an effect over time.

Epilogue

Fifteen hundred years ago, everybody knew that the Earth was the center of the universe. Five hundred years ago, everybody knew that the Earth was flat. And fifteen minutes ago, you knew that humans were alone on this planet. Imagine what you'll know tomorrow.[41]

In the Prologue I stated that I would approach this work with Occam's Razor in mind; i.e., the simplest explanations are most likely correct. The problem is that what we think are the simplest explanations are based on our current level of understanding. As a physicist working in quantum field theory, I found it somewhat mystifying that the most accurate theories we have for predicting the results of measurements are also philosophically untenable, or as a minimum, call into question our understanding of reality. Our inability to reconcile quantum field theory and general relativity has led us to increasingly abstract conceptions of what reality might be – unobserved extra dimensions, a simulation, a multiverse, a holographic universe, and more.

I've based most of our conversation so far on *simple physical* concepts, and along those lines I've portrayed the human brain as a collection of biological computers (or at least two, as in our two-computer model). And I've claimed that our *feeling* of consciousness arises as a result of recursive processes akin to Hofstadter's "strange loop" (recall Escher's Drawing Hands).

The physicist in me would say that as far as we know, the universe, including us, is composed of a collection of particles and their interactions. If we possess consciousness as a result of those physical systems, then maybe the universe has a consciousness too. One of the founders of quantum mechanics, Erwin Schrödinger, in fact believed that there is only one mind in the universe, and we are all just part of it.[42] The universe is, by some descriptions,[43] a very large information processing "computer".

In describing these ideas to my wife Vicky, her reply was simply "I don't want to be just a computer". And quite honestly, neither do I. I confess that I believe in something more. I also confess right up front, I don't understand death...and I guess by extension, I don't understand life – the why. And if we're all being honest, I don't think anyone does. I can't reconcile eternity nor finality, living forever or the permanence of death. Our concept of time presents us with this dilemma.

Finally, I confess I have no answers. This book and my explorations are intended to connect my struggles with this subject with your own, and to underscore the fact that we all face the same questions. It's the human condition that we all share, and hopefully by sharing it more openly we can all become more compassionate.

So with that in mind, and with my readers indulgence, I'd like to take this opportunity to explore some alternative concepts.

Throughout history, philosophers (and most people maybe unknowingly) have wrestled with the "body-mind problem". In the simplest terms, if we want the mind to be somehow independent of the body (existing beyond the body like a soul), then the question becomes how can something non-physical affect something physical? Or conversely, how can a physical system give rise to conscious experience – a somehow non-physical essence? (This is the "hard problem" as posed by Chalmers.[44])

So let's begin our exploration by revisiting the two-computer model (referring again to Figure 2 and the surrounding dialogue). Computer 1 has all the ingredients to fully operate a person. As viewed from the outside, we would likely have difficulty distinguishing a person with no Computer 2 from another who has a Computer 2. We can imagine a sophisticated system of algorithms that would fool most of us. (This is somewhat akin to Chalmer's zombies.[45]) Computer 2 is "watching the movie" produced by Computer 1, and although Computer 2 can interpret, interact with, and redirect Computer 1's operations, Computer 1 (our subconscious brain) operates the body. Studies have indicated, in fact, that in many cases our conscious awareness of a decision to act occurs after the action.

If we take seriously the factoring of body and mind, as represented, for example, by the two-computer model, then I propose four possible scenarios:

1. Computer 1 and Computer 2 are both physical entities, as described in this book, and there is

a physical connection between them, and consciousness arises from a purely physical process like recursion.

2. Computer 1 is physical, but Computer 2 is non-physical, or at least beyond our current understanding of physics as is the connection between them.

3. Computer 2 is physical, but Computer 1 is non-physical.

4. Both Computer 1 and Computer 2 are non-physical or beyond our current understanding of physics.

Here, just to underscore, when I say non-physical I simply mean beyond our current understanding of physics or reality. If, for example, reality was found to be a "simulation", then I would categorize it as non-physical – at least for our present discussion.

We've explored the first scenario in some detail in this book. And although there might be other physical mechanisms for how consciousness arises (as referenced herein), they are, nonetheless, founded on our current understanding of physics. In this case, the perceived independence of mind and body arises as illustrated in the two-computer model. That is, since Computer 1 operates the body and presents Computer 2 with models (for example, distilled from sense data), it *feels* as though there is a separation of mind from body. And the recursive nature between the two allows us to perceive that separation.

Now, even though scenario 1 is based on a physical interpretation of reality, we don't necessarily understand all that's implied. Our thoughts on consciousness and how it arises are evolving, and we're not entirely clear on what constitutes consciousness. It could in fact be that the entire universe is a conscious *god-like thing* and we are simply part of it. It's even possible that the universe *is* an information processing entity not unlike a computer.

The second scenario implies that Computer 2, and in fact the linkage between Computer 1 and Computer 2, is somehow beyond our current understanding. This scenario is the belief that there is a physical universe, but our consciousness somehow transcends the physical and takes on a spiritual existence. Our mind /

spiritual being is bound to our bodies and is released on death. This is foundational in much of our mythology and religion. A significant amount of research has been devoted to finding evidence for extensions of mind beyond body and / or spiritual existence beyond body. And although there doesn't appear to be scientifically verified evidence, there is a significant body of anecdotal experience that maintains this scenario of reality.

Near-death experiences, for example, have been recounted with a perceived separation from the body on death – the so called "out-of-body experience". I use the term *perceived* here because, as we've discussed previously, this could also be the result of Computer 1 presenting a model of the death event like a vision or dream, and could likewise be applied to scenario 1.

It might, in fact, be that evolution has furnished us with a mechanism by which the final moments of life *feel* like a heavenly eternity – a vision in which time stands still. As a result of our evolution, our brains are conditioned to predict the near-term future and to protect us from being overwhelmed by information. The prospect of death could trigger such a defense mechanism. Nevertheless, the fact that many of those experiencing near-death relate similar stories is, in the least, intriguing.

I listed scenario 3 for completeness, but I'm not sure how to proceed with the thought process other than to say it would mean that our minds are somehow physical, but everything else is illusion or non-physical. It calls into question then what is the physical substance or vessel of the mind?

Scenario 4 is the idea that our reality is somehow an illusion. As I mentioned previously, all of our information about the external world comes to our brains and minds via sense data. The origins of that data may not be actual physical sources. Our reality (including our physical bodies) could be a "simulation".

This is likely somewhat disconcerting as it begs the question who created the simulation and why? But it is also not inconsistent with our creation mythology. The questions of how the universe, and we, came to be and why are still outstanding and may never be answered.

My list is likely not exhaustive, but illustrates the utility of pursuing the boundary between physics and spirituality. We each get to choose our version of reality based on our *beliefs*. I believe there is much that is beyond our current understanding, and can see the potential for any of these scenarios to be true. Our notions of time and space have in many ways placed limitations on our ability to conceive of how alternatives might fit into our belief systems. The keys are to recognize beliefs for what they are; better understand the origins of our thoughts, opinions, and our vulnerability; and become more conscious and compassionate humans.

My goal in this work was to encourage empathy and emotional growth of our society by exploring how we think, learn, and communicate. In my opinion these are the primary elements of the human condition that we're all experiencing. My hope is that by reading this you've gained some understanding and compassion for yourself and others.

Groundhog Day

By bang or wave of hand
Our universe came to be
Unique or one of many
It matters not to me

My fate is yours and yours is mine
Our futures are entwined
We walk this road together
Regardless of our kind

We are, you see, all one and so
We might as well enjoy it
The alternative is suffering
And I, for one, abhor it

About the Author

A polymath of diverse talents and a passionate learner and teacher, Michael has woven an extraordinary tapestry throughout his career. Starting in the culinary field, he worked as a chef at numerous restaurants and hotels around the country and made his mark by winning first place at the Southeastern food show in Atlanta. His academic endeavors began with the study of philosophy and computer science before venturing into the realm of theoretical physics, where his insatiable curiosity and analytical mind earned him a Ph.D. in theoretical nuclear physics and led to nineteen publications in refereed journals on the structure of the atomic nucleus. Transitioning into the aerospace industry, he completed executive education courses in finance at Wharton and strategy at the Brookings Institution. He rose to the role of Vice President, channeling his passion for innovation and education to help drive the company's advancement, before retiring early to pursue new interests. Ever an advocate for learning, as a lecturer of both physics and business, in just his second year after retirement he was voted faculty of the year by MBA students at the Milgard Business School at the University of Washington. He tirelessly shares his knowledge, mentors aspiring minds, and champions the unlocking of human potential, epitomizing a life dedicated to the pursuit of excellence in various spheres.

Notes and References

[1] This is a simplification of Maslow's work. Abraham Maslow, a prominent psychologist in the mid-20th century, is best known for his groundbreaking work on fundamental motives and human motivation. He developed the famous hierarchy of needs, a psychological theory that outlines a pyramid of human needs arranged in ascending order of importance. At the base of the pyramid are physiological needs such as food and shelter, followed by safety, love and belonging, esteem, and self-actualization at the pinnacle. Maslow believed that individuals strive to fulfill these needs in a sequential manner, with higher-level motives becoming relevant once lower-level needs are met. His work revolutionized the field of psychology by emphasizing the importance of understanding human motivation and well-being in a holistic and hierarchical context. Maslow's insights continue to influence various disciplines, including psychology, sociology, and management, providing valuable insights into what drives human behavior and personal development.

2 Consciousness, often regarded as the subjective experience of the mind, is a concept deeply explored by philosophers and neuroscientists alike. David Chalmers, a prominent figure in the field of philosophy of mind, has notably contributed to the discourse on consciousness. He introduced the idea of the "hard problem of consciousness," highlighting that while we can explain the brain's mechanisms and functions, the subjective nature of conscious experience itself remains a profound mystery. This subjectivity is what sets consciousness apart, as it encapsulates our unique perspectives, emotions, and awareness. Chalmers' work reminds us that understanding consciousness goes beyond mere neural processes and touches upon the essence of what it means to have an inner world, emphasizing the intricate nature of this subjective phenomenon.

3 Moore's Law, formulated by Gordon E. Moore, co-founder of Intel Corporation, in 1965, is a seminal principle in the field of computer science and technology. This law predicted that the number of transistors on a microchip would double approximately every two years, while the cost of computing would decrease. Moore's Law has held remarkably true for several decades, driving the relentless pace of innovation in the electronics industry. It has enabled the continuous miniaturization of microchips, leading to exponential increases in computing power, efficiency, and the development of smaller, more powerful electronic devices. This exponential growth has had profound implications for industries ranging from personal computing and telecommunications to artificial intelligence and scientific research. While there are challenges to sustaining this trend due to physical limitations, Moore's Law has left an indelible mark on the evolution of technology and continues to shape our increasingly connected and digital world.

[4] Ornstein, R. (1992). *Evolution of consciousness: The Origins of the Way We Think.* Simon and Schuster.

[5] Hofstadter, D. R. (2007). *I am a strange loop.* Basic Books.

[6] Koch, C. (2019). *The feeling of life itself: Why Consciousness Is Widespread but Can't Be Computed.* MIT Press.

[7] Graziano, M. S. A. (2019b). *Rethinking consciousness: A Scientific Theory of Subjective Experience.* National Geographic Books.

[8] Here I'm referring to the Star Trek: The Next Generation episode titled "Darmok," which is a fan-favorite. In this episode, Captain Jean-Luc Picard encounters the enigmatic Tamarians, who communicate solely through metaphors drawn from their own history and mythology. The central challenge of the episode lies in Picard's efforts to bridge the gap between their radically different linguistic styles. Through shared experiences and trials, Picard gradually begins to grasp the Tamarian metaphors, leading to a breakthrough in understanding and cooperation. "Darmok" explores themes of language, communication, and the universal human desire to find common ground with others, even in the face of seemingly insurmountable differences. It remains a memorable and thought-provoking installment in the Star Trek series.

[9] Jung, *Collected Works* vol. 8 (1960), "Instinct and the Unconscious" (1919/1948), 268–269 (pp. 131–132). Note: Jung refers to *Pronuba yucasella*, now apparently classified as *Tegeticula yucasella*. See also: "The Yucca and Its Moth", *The Prairie Ecologist*, 8 December 2010.

[10] Descartes, R. (1979). *Meditations on first Philosophy: In which the Existence of God and the Distinction of the Soul from the Body are Demonstrated.* Hackett Publishing Company.

[11] The idea that we might be residents in a computer simulation is a concept explored in philosophy and speculative science fiction, popularized in part by philosopher Nick Bostrom's simulation hypothesis. This hypothesis suggests that if an advanced civilization were capable of creating highly realistic simulations of reality, it would be statistically more likely that we exist within one of those simulations rather than in the base physical reality.

However, it's important to emphasize that this is a theoretical and philosophical idea, not a proven scientific fact. Currently, there is no empirical evidence to confirm or refute the simulation hypothesis. It remains a subject of philosophical debate and speculation rather than a widely accepted scientific theory.

Most scientists and researchers continue to focus on explaining the universe and its existence within the framework of established physical laws and principles. While the simulation hypothesis is intriguing and raises profound questions about the nature of reality, it has not been substantiated by scientific evidence.

12 The "mind-body problem" is a central issue in philosophy and cognitive science that concerns the relationship between the physical body and the human mind or consciousness. It asks how mental experiences, thoughts, and subjective awareness arise from the physical processes of the brain and body. Various theories have been proposed to address this problem, ranging from dualism (which posits a fundamental separation between the mind and body) to materialism (which asserts that all mental phenomena can be explained by physical processes). The mind-body problem has profound implications for our understanding of consciousness, identity, and the nature of reality, and it continues to be a subject of active debate and research across multiple disciplines, including philosophy, neuroscience, psychology, and artificial intelligence.

13 This concept was explored in some detail by Graziano. See Chapter 9 in Graziano, M. S. A. (2019b). *Rethinking consciousness: A Scientific Theory of Subjective Experience*. National Geographic Books.

[14] Layers in artificial neural networks can be categorized into input, hidden, and output layers. Input layers receive data, which is then processed through one or more hidden layers, where intricate computations occur. Each layer consists of numerous interconnected artificial neurons, and these connections, known as weights, are adjusted through a training process to optimize the network's performance. The layers create a hierarchical representation of information, with each subsequent layer extracting increasingly abstract features or patterns from the input data. This layering technique allows neural networks to model complex relationships in data and make predictions or classifications, making them a cornerstone of modern machine learning and artificial intelligence applications.

[15] A flip-flop is a fundamental building block of digital electronic circuits, and it serves as a crucial memory element. Think of it as a tiny switch that can be in one of two states, either on or off, representing binary values (0 or 1). Flip-flops are commonly used to store and synchronize data within digital systems. They can be thought of as a basic form of memory, capable of holding a single bit of information until it's updated. Flip-flops are the backbone of sequential logic in computer processors, enabling them to perform tasks like arithmetic, logic operations, and data storage. These circuits play a foundational role in modern electronics, ensuring the proper flow and storage of data in a synchronized manner.

[16] Penrose, R. (1999). *The Emperor's new mind: Concerning Computers, Minds, and the Laws of Physics.* Oxford Paperbacks.

[17] Kurt Gödel's assertion that any formal system can be modeled by integers is a foundational concept in mathematical logic and the study of formal systems. Known as Gödel numbering or arithmetization, this idea involves encoding the symbols, syntax, and structure of a formal system into unique integers. By doing so, Gödel demonstrated that even abstract, complex mathematical and logical systems could be represented within the framework of arithmetic. This remarkable insight allowed him to formulate his famous incompleteness theorems, which showed that no consistent formal system could prove its own consistency. Gödel's work illustrated the power of mathematical representation and paved the way for a deeper understanding of the limits and intricacies of formal logic, influencing fields ranging from computer science to philosophy. It also underscored the universality and versatility of the integer-based numerical system in describing the complexities of human thought and formal reasoning.

[18] See Ornstein Section III. Ornstein, R. (1992). *Evolution of consciousness: The Origins of the Way We Think*. Simon and Schuster.

[19] See Hofstadter Chapter 3. Hofstadter, D. R. (2007). *I am a strange loop*. Basic Books.

[20] Levine, S. (2010). *A gradual awakening*. Anchor.

[21] Tolle, E. (1999). *The power of now: A Guide to Spiritual Enlightenment*. New World Library.

22 Albert Einstein's thought experiments were instrumental in his development of groundbreaking theories in physics. These mental exercises allowed him to explore complex concepts, often involving space, time, and the behavior of light, without the need for elaborate physical experiments. One of his most famous thought experiments involved the theory of special relativity, where he imagined what would happen if someone rode a beam of light. This led to the development of his theory of relativity, which transformed our understanding of space and time. Einstein's ability to visualize and conceptualize abstract physics concepts through thought experiments was a testament to his creative genius and played a pivotal role in reshaping the foundations of modern physics. These imaginative mental exercises continue to inspire scientists and students alike, highlighting the power of thought and imagination in scientific discovery.

23 Devaney, R. L. (1986). An introduction to chaotic dynamical systems. Addison Wesley Publishing Company.

24 See Veritasium. https://www.veritasium.com

25 Kahneman, D. (2011). Thinking, fast and slow. Farrar, Straus and Giroux.

Epistemology is a branch of philosophy that delves into the study of knowledge, its nature, and the processes by which we acquire it. It explores fundamental questions about what can be considered knowledge, how we can be certain about what we know, and the distinctions between belief, opinion, and justified true belief. Epistemologists investigate the reliability of various sources of knowledge, such as perception, reason, testimony, and introspection, while also examining concepts like skepticism, justification, and the nature of truth. This field plays a crucial role in shaping our understanding of the boundaries of human knowledge and the methods we use to acquire and evaluate information, making it a foundational discipline for philosophy and a wide range of other intellectual pursuits.

²⁷ Marginal value theory, often associated with economics, refers to the concept that the value or utility of an additional unit of a resource or good (the marginal unit) decreases as the quantity of that resource or good increases. It's a fundamental principle in microeconomics and decision-making, influencing choices ranging from consumption to production. According to this theory, individuals or firms allocate resources to maximize their overall satisfaction or profit by comparing the additional benefit (marginal utility) of obtaining one more unit of a good with the additional cost (marginal cost) of acquiring it. Marginal value theory plays a crucial role in understanding how individuals make choices in a world of limited resources and helps explain phenomena such as price determination, consumer preferences, and production optimization in economic contexts.

The Marginal Value Theorem is a fundamental concept in the field of behavioral ecology and foraging theory. Developed by ecologist Eric Charnov in 1976, this theorem provides insights into how animals should make foraging decisions in environments where resources are distributed unevenly. It posits that an animal should leave a resource patch and move to a new one when the rate of energy gain in the current patch drops below the average rate of gain for the entire environment. In other words, it helps to determine when an animal should stop exploiting a particular resource and move on to optimize its foraging strategy. The Marginal Value Theorem has applications in understanding the behavior of various species in the wild, from birds foraging for food to predators hunting prey, shedding

[28] Profit is maximized when the marginal revenue equals the marginal cost. To see this, consider the expression for profit (P) in terms of revenue (R) and cost (C); i.e., P=R-C. Then taking the derivative of P with respect to the number of units and setting it equal to zero gives P'=R'-C'=0 or R'=C'.

[29] To see this, let p=P/n be the average profit where P is the profit and n is the number of units. Then p=(R-C)/n where again R is revenue and C is cost. Taking the derivative of p with respect to n and setting p' equal to zero yields p=P' or average profit equals marginal profit.

[30] My wife Vicky illustrated the difference between facts and opinions as: when I say its cold outside that's an opinion and when I say its 20 degrees (F) outside that's a fact.

[31] The Socratic method, named after the ancient Greek philosopher Socrates, is a time-honored approach to philosophical inquiry and critical thinking. Socrates' method involves engaging in open-ended, question-and-answer dialogues to stimulate intellectual exploration and draw out deeper insights. Instead of providing direct answers, Socrates used a series of probing questions to encourage his interlocutors to examine their beliefs, assumptions, and knowledge. This dialectical method aims to uncover contradictions, clarify concepts, and arrive at a more profound understanding of a subject. The Socratic method has had a lasting influence on education, law, and philosophy, emphasizing the importance of active inquiry, self-examination, and the pursuit of truth through reasoned discourse. It continues to be a valuable tool for fostering critical thinking and encouraging a deeper exploration of complex ideas and moral values.

"Power of Myth" by Joseph Campbell is a profound exploration of the enduring role of myths and storytelling in human culture. Through engaging conversations with journalist Bill Moyers, Campbell delves into the universal themes and symbols that shape our understanding of the world. The book highlights how myths transcend time and culture, revealing common threads that connect humanity's spiritual and cultural traditions. Campbell's insights into the hero's journey and the hero's role in mythology have had a profound impact on literature, filmmaking, and the arts, inspiring countless creators to craft narratives that resonate with the human experience. "Power of Myth" invites readers to contemplate the timeless wisdom contained within ancient stories and their relevance to our lives today, emphasizing the enduring power of storytelling to illuminate the human condition.

[33] ChatGPT is an advanced AI language model developed by OpenAI. It's built upon the GPT-3.5 architecture and is designed to engage in natural language conversations with users. ChatGPT is renowned for its ability to understand and generate human-like text responses, making it highly versatile and valuable for a wide range of applications. Whether it's answering questions, providing explanations, assisting with creative writing, or offering general conversation, ChatGPT can provide informative and contextually relevant responses. While it can be a valuable tool for various tasks, it's essential to remember that ChatGPT generates responses based on patterns in the data it was trained on and does not possess consciousness or true understanding. It's a powerful AI language model that showcases the advancements in natural language processing and has the potential to enhance productivity and assist users in diverse ways. Some elements of this work were written with the aid of ChatGPT including this citation.

[34] See Ornstein Section II. Ornstein, R. (1992). *Evolution of consciousness: The Origins of the Way We Think*. Simon and Schuster.

[35] See Joseph Campbell Wikipedia page https://en.wikipedia.org/wiki/Joseph_Campbell

[36] Maslow, A. H. (1998). *Toward a psychology of being*. John Wiley & Sons.

[37] Frankl, V. E. (2006). *Man's search for meaning*. Beacon Press.

[38] Browning, C. R. (2017). *Ordinary men: Reserve Police Battalion 101 and the Final Solution in Poland*. Harper Perennial.

39 See Roots of Empathy. https://rootsofempathy.org

40 Frank, Michael Ruhl (2019). *Axioms on leadership: A Companion Guide for Developing Leaders.* Independently Published.

41 "Men in Black" is a popular science fiction comedy film directed by Barry Sonnenfeld, released in 1997. The movie stars Will Smith and Tommy Lee Jones as Agents J and K, who are members of a top-secret organization known as the Men in Black (MIB). Their mission is to monitor and regulate extraterrestrial activity on Earth while keeping it hidden from the public.

The iconic scene in "Men in Black" where Agent J and Agent K are sitting on a bench takes place in Central Park. Agent J, still grappling with the shock of discovering aliens and their role as Men in Black, asks Agent K about the truth behind the organization and the secrecy surrounding it. Agent K, in his trademark deadpan style, responds, "A person is smart. People are dumb, panicky, dangerous animals, and you know it. Fifteen hundred years ago everybody knew the Earth was the center of the universe. Five hundred years ago, everybody knew the Earth was flat, and fifteen minutes ago, you knew that humans were alone on this planet. Imagine what you'll know tomorrow." This quote encapsulates the film's underlying theme of the general public's ignorance and vulnerability when faced with the reality of extraterrestrial life. Agent K's wisdom and experience shine through, emphasizing the need for secrecy and control in handling the truth about aliens. This scene is not only memorable for its humor but also for the philosophical perspective it offers on the human reaction to the unknown.

42 Schrödinger, E. 1. (2021). *Mind and matter.* --. Hassell Street Press.

43 Viewing the universe as a computer is a concept rooted in theoretical physics and cosmology, particularly within the framework of digital physics. This idea suggests that the fundamental processes governing the universe, including the behavior of particles and the evolution of physical laws, can be described and modeled computationally. Proponents of this notion argue that the universe operates like a vast, complex computation, with the laws of physics serving as its underlying code. This perspective has led to intriguing discussions about the nature of reality, the simulation hypothesis, and the possibility that advanced civilizations or entities could simulate universes within supercomputers. While it's a thought-provoking hypothesis, it remains speculative and has not been empirically confirmed. Nevertheless, the idea of the universe as a computer underscores the deep interplay between science, computation, and the quest to understand the fundamental workings of our cosmos.

⁴⁴ The "hard problem" of consciousness, a term coined by philosopher David Chalmers, refers to the profound and perplexing issue at the heart of understanding consciousness. While neuroscience can explain the mechanisms of brain function and how it correlates with certain conscious experiences, it falls short of explaining why and how physical processes in the brain give rise to subjective, qualitative experiences, often referred to as "qualia." This problem delves into the mystery of why we have inner thoughts, emotions, and a vivid sense of self. It challenges our conventional understanding of the physical world, leading to debates about whether consciousness is fundamentally irreducible to physical processes or if there exists a yet-to-be-discovered scientific explanation for this enigma. The hard problem of consciousness remains a central puzzle in philosophy and neuroscience, raising profound questions about the nature of our existence and the limits of scientific inquiry.

⁴⁵ Chalmers proposed that it is conceivable, at least in a thought experiment, that there could exist beings that are physically identical to humans but lack consciousness. These zombies would behave exactly like conscious humans, yet they would have no subjective experiences or inner awareness. Chalmers used this idea to highlight the apparent gap in our understanding of how physical processes in the brain give rise to conscious experience. Philosophical zombies challenge traditional materialistic views of the mind and encourage contemplation on what distinguishes physical processes from conscious awareness. While they are a hypothetical construct, Chalmers' zombies have been influential in discussions about the nature of consciousness and the limits of scientific explanation in this field.

ISBN: 9789635245482

Made in United States
North Haven, CT
06 September 2025

72571954R00095